D1384038

The sociology
of the
school curriculum

John Eggleston
Professor of Education
University of Keele

The sociology
of the
school curriculum

LB
15 70
. E 385

Routledge & Kegan Paul
London, Henley and Boston

INDIANA
PURDUE
LIBRARY
JAN 30 1979
FORT WAYNE

WITHDRAWN

First published in 1977
by Routledge &Kegan Paul Ltd
39 Store Street,
London WC1E 7DD,
Broadway House,
Newtown Road,
Henley-on-Thames,
Oxon RG9 1EN and
9 Park Street,
Boston, Mass. 02108, USA
Set in IBM Press Roman by
Express Litho Service (Oxford)
and printed in Great Britain by
Unwin Brothers Ltd
The Gresham Press, Old Woking, Surrey
A member of the Staples Printing Group
© John Eggleston 1977

No part of this book may be reproduced in
any form without permission from the
publisher, except for the quotation of brief
passages in criticism

British Library Cataloguing in Publication Data

Eggleston, John

The sociology of the school curriculum.

1. Education — Great Britain — Curricula
I. Title
375p.00941   LB1564.G7

ISBN 0-7100-8565-6
ISBN 0-7100-8566-4 Pbk.

Contents

Preface

This book has taken a 'long time in the writing'. Curriculum is a complex set of human behaviours and understandings that is surrounded by an atmosphere of intimate accounts of the action and a stratosphere of philosophy. To break through these layers and reach an interrelated account of curriculum behaviour, consciousness and ideology in a sociological perspective is a difficult task. But even though sources have not always been helpful, colleagues have been unfailingly so. Out of many I would particularly like to thank Marjorie Cruickshank, Denis Gleeson, Geoff Powell and Philip Robinson for their helpful comments on the manuscript. I owe a similar debt to Barbara Wiggins, Catherine Mitchell, Jane Cordingley and Mary McBratney for their equally valuable help in preparing the manuscript and to the staff of the Keele Institute of Education Library for chasing elusive references. I am also grateful to Rachel Sharp and Tony Green for allowing me to use excerpts from their book *Education and Social Control*. Needless to say, I owe the errors and omissions to no one but myself.

JE

Introduction

After a century of compulsory education for all, the achievements of the schools are subject to fundamental questions, not only by educators but also by governments, industrialists and parents.

There is a widespread belief that, far from being instruments of change, schools have reinforced existing social systems and legitimated longstanding distributions of power and status. Moreover, they are alleged to have failed to respond to the economic and technological imperatives of the late twentieth century.

The ensuing analysis of schooling has taken many forms but a central focus is the curriculum, its knowledge content and the way in which that content is determined, evaluated and made available.

Yet though the curriculum is being subjected to extensive scrutiny, there has been little specifically sociological examination; sociological approaches to the curriculum have tended to be narrow, concerned with limited areas or to have been based on a single ideological perspective.

The purpose of this book is to remedy some of the deficiencies and to present a distinctive and wide ranging sociological analysis of the curriculum as an aid to an understanding of the present state of the school curriculum and the issues of social control that surround it. It attempts to answer such questions as who decides what is to be taught, why is there a status hierarchy of curriculum knowledge, why some pupils are effectively excluded from some areas of knowledge, but admitted to others. In short, it looks at the nature of curriculum experience of teachers and students, its availability to them, their response to it and the consequences for them. In doing so it provides a sociological accompaniment to the analyses of curriculum currently being undertaken throughout western society.

1 Sociology and the curriculum

What is considered to be 'knowledge' in a society? Equally importantly, what is regarded as 'non-knowledge'? In most societies with schools one of the best places to look for answers to these questions is in the curricula used in the classrooms. Here we can find not only many examples of the knowledge that is socially approved but also some of the 'legitimating ideologies' that lie behind it.

The diversity of patterns of approved knowledge was early noted by Mannheim who in *Ideology and Utopia* asked:

> How is it possible that identical human thought processes concerned with the same world produce different conceptions of that world? . . . Is it not possible that the thought processes which are involved here are not at all identical? May it not be found, when one has examined all the possibilities of human thought, that there are numerous alternative patterns which can be followed?

There are many examples of fundamental differences in thought processes. North American Indians have, for the most part, no way of saying 'why' in the characteristic manner of the North American whites. For them the crucial question in the consideration of events is 'how did it happen?'. The difference is fundamental. For the Indian, knowledge is the accumulation of material that is believed to be explanatory. For the white, knowledge is the accumulation of answers that are believed to be rational.

Knowledge and culture

Differences in thought processes and the differences in the perception of events that ensue lead to differences in the store of knowledge possessed by each society and by each group. These stores of knowledge

1

transmitted from generation to generation with only gradual modification form the *culture* of societies and groups. Indeed it is culture that identifies not only societies but also tribes, nations, races, social classes and most of the other semi-permanent groups of social life. Components of culture may include attitudes to one's fellow men in and out of the group, appropriate perceptions of the economic system, dietary restrictions, work ethics, religious and political beliefs as well as a whole series of what Schutz (1967) has called *recipe book knowledge* consisting mainly of rule-of-thumb formulae which can be applied in a routine way to everyday situations. Culture with its basis of stored, shared, valid and legitimate knowledge constitutes the accepted way of life in a group. The learning and internalization of at least an essential core of the culture by each individual is seen to be an essential prelude to achieving a recognized adult identity or, as Durkheim puts it, 'to construct the social being'. It may also be necessary for the individual to learn variations of the culture or *sub-cultures* — stores of knowledge that are required, over and above the common culture, in order to achieve full membership of a group such as a student society, a youth club or a school staffroom. Such knowledge may include understanding the subtleties of dress, the acquisition of 'in speech' and the learning of approved work norms. Structures of sub-cultural groups such as Dennis, Henriques and Slaughter's (1957) study of a mining community show clearly how sharply different are the sub-cultural definitions of knowledge between different communities and how rigidly these definitions are maintained — between, for example, the definition of men's work and women's work. The relationship between the shared perceptions of knowledge and individual behaviour are at the heart of the definition of culture and sub-culture.

Transmission and legitimation

But in both culture and sub-culture it is important to identify not only the knowledge content but the ways in which it is defined at any given moment as valid, correct, proper and generally unquestionable — in other words as being *legitimate*.

All societies have processes not only to ensure the storage and transmission of knowledge but also to make certain that its definition becomes internalized by the young. In pre-industrial societies such processes were conducted by church, community and family. These institutions transmitted appropriate religious beliefs, stratification principles, agrarian and military skills, procreational and child-rearing practices; often holding an initiation ceremony to mark the successful transmission of the most central aspects of the knowledge. In industrial societies such *socialization* came to require supplementations.

The increasing complexity of knowledge needed by all members — literacy and numeracy — in order to perform adult occupational roles occurred at a time when the strength of church and community was diminished by migration to the new industrial areas. But the problems of industrialization were not confined to the transmission and legitimation of occupational knowledge. The movement to the towns, through weakening the strength of the socialization of the established communities, weakened the hold of community definitions of knowledge such as consensus norms of living together, definitions of differences, rights and responsibilities, the rule of law and much else. Moreover, new definitions appropriate to the mass society rather than to the local community were called for. To achieve all this the school and its curriculum were called upon to become an essential instrument in the transmission and legitimation of knowledge in the industrial society. In short, to become instruments of *social control* that help to ensure the maintenance of the social system — its knowledge, its status, stratification and above all its power.

Distribution and evaluation of knowledge

Yet knowledge is not only defined, transmitted and legitimated in all societies, it is also distributed. Every society makes different amounts and kinds of knowledge available to different categories of members. Some areas of knowledge may be sacred or private and careful selection may take place before access to them is allowed (Bernstein, 1975). Still other areas may allow the exercise of great power when possessed and here there may be rules to determine the struggle to attain them. Furthermore, knowledge is evaluated; medical and legal knowledge is characteristically accorded high status; manual skills, especially of a routine nature, are usually accorded lower status as are those who exercise them. The distribution of knowledge is also a feature of sub-cultures as the study by Dennis, Henriques and Slaughter (1957) clearly showed. Patrol leaders in scouting attend separate courses from ordinary scouts to receive knowledge that is not available to ordinary scouts, headteachers receive information from local education administrators that cannot be divulged to ordinary teachers. Their power is redefined or reinforced in consequence.

In all these matters the school curriculum takes on major responsibilities. As Musgrave (1972) has noted, 'curriculum stands analytically at the centre of the process whereby any society manages its stock of knowledge'. The distribution aspects of the school curriculum are amongst its most obvious characteristics — different curricula being available not only to children of different age and sex but also to those for whom teachers attribute differences in ability, prospects or propensity to use knowledge. The judgments made by teachers in this and all other aspects of curriculum must themselves of course be seen in the context of the definition of knowledge within the society in which they teach and the professional sub-cultures of which they are members.

Curriculum studies

Yet despite such abundant justification for a sociological study of the curriculum, until recently there has been remarkably little attention given to the curriculum by sociologists, who have tended to take it as a 'given' feature of the school systems they have studied in their investigations of socialization, differential opportunity and classroom interaction. The early encouragement of Mannheim for a sociology of education based upon the sociology of knowledge was not taken up.

The rapid development of 'curriculum studies' and 'curriculum theory' that can be seen throughout the contemporary literature of education has arisen from other, predominantly non-sociological sources. It springs, in the main, from the large-scale programmes of re-examination, renewal and revision of the school curriculum currently taking place on the initiatives of teachers, local education authorities, professional organizations and sponsoring bodies such as Schools Council and the Nuffield Foundation. Such programmes have commonly responded to pressing needs in the schools, most notably in the secondary schools faced with such problems as comprehensive reorganization and the raising of the school-leaving age. But the apparent redefinition of many areas of curriculum knowledge has also been a factor for change. It is argued that the content of scientific knowledge changes in an age of electronics; the content of mathematics changes in an age of computers; the content of language changes in an age of mass communication. Associated with these changes in the definition of content there are also believed to be changes in the appropriate distribution of knowledge to the individual. In the recent past it was believed that the curriculum should 'stock up' the individual with appropriate knowledge (facts, skills and values) that would stand him in good stead throughout the adult life anticipated for him. This was a belief based upon the assumption that adult roles changed only slowly and the knowledge needs of existing generations of adults could therefore be used as a reasonable guide to the requirements of the emergent generations. Many educators assert that, in contemporary society, not only does knowledge appear to change more rapidly but also that there are more efficient and less costly methods of storing it than in the memory of the individual. In consequence, the emphasis of curriculum is seen to shift to the individual as a knowledge developer and user rather than as a walking storage system. The educator's objectives for his curriculum tend to be expressed increasingly in terms not of remembering but of creating, discovering, and inventing. Such approaches implicitly — yet seldom explicitly — seem to suggest that the social control function of the curriculum is being diminished, that instead individual determination is being fostered along the lines of the Durkheimian shift from 'mechanical' to 'organic' social solidarity.

Yet despite the unmistakable sociological assumptions associated with these and many other views of curriculum and their widespread endorsement by teachers, both the practice and the 'theoretical developments' that have sprung from them have been for the most part devoid of sociological analysis. In consequence the study of the curriculum has usually lacked an adequate consideration of either the social factors that influence it or the social implications to which it gives rise both within the school and in the society at large. Many of the so-called models of curriculum change in particular imply a set of sociological assumptions that are surprisingly naive. Some imply a degree of consensus concerning aims of the curriculum that, even amongst teachers, is patently untrue. Still others imply a possibility of curriculum change merely through the manipulation of content and methodology. With such a slender basis of sociological analysis the possible consequences and even the very feasibility of new curriculum approaches can only be incompletely examined as was clearly to be seen in the first Open University curriculum units *The Curriculum: Context Design and Development* (1972). The somewhat greater sociological content in the revised course is reflected in the two course readers (Harris, Lawn and Prescott, 1976, and Goldby, Greenwald and West, 1976).

Sociological initiatives

It is not difficult to find reasons for these omissions by sociologists. For many years their preoccupation with selective processes gave rise to a situation in which the content of the curriculum was largely ignored (even though the differentiation of pupils was often seen to be achieved through differentiated curricula).

But in more recent years the situation has changed very rapidly. A number of sociologists have produced papers that review the areas in which a sociological perspective may be applied to the study of what is taught in schools. In consequence the curriculum has come to be seen more clearly as an important instrument, if not the most important instrument, in the process whereby the school helps the young to assume adult roles. More importantly, the curriculum is also viewed as a central factor in the establishment and maintenance of the power and authority structures both of the society and the school. In consequence sociologists have become interested not only in curriculum content, method and evaluation, but also in the origins and support of the implicit and explicit values that are embodied in the curriculum. They are interested in how the curriculum is legitimated, in why decisions, both overt and covert, are made as they are and in the social factors that determine the choice of subjects and their content and method. As Bernstein (1971) has put it, the sociologist now wishes to explore the ways in which a society selects, classifies, transmits and evaluates its 'public' knowledge. This brings us to the heart of the matter — the view of the school curriculum as one of the important instruments through which the prevailing features of a society's cultural system are carried; wherein its knowledge is transmitted and evaluated.

This new interest of sociologists in the curriculum is of course closely linked with the renewed interest in the sociology of knowledge itself. Here particular attention centres on the renewed emphasis that the nature of knowledge is not fixed and unalterable but rather a consequence of the perceptions of individuals. These further moves from a positivist view of knowledge to a reflexive one open up highly interesting questions concerning the legitimation of knowledge and in particular the legitimation of the curriculum. Alongside these new approaches there have also been sociological explorations of curriculum ideologies and decision-making procedures and some valuable work on the classification of curricula. Information on the history of both 'traditional' and 'progressive' curricula has also become more fully available and alongside this case studies on the processes of 'curriculum innovation' have been undertaken.

The orientations of this volume

This book seeks to bring together and build upon the various sociological initiatives in the study of the curriculum. It also seeks to juxtapose them against the wide range of non-sociological initiatives. In so doing it hopes to throw light on the present encompassing debates on education — the debates on its purposes, its organization, its methods, its achievements and even the desirability of its continued existence.

What are the ways in which a sociologist may begin his analysis of the school curriculum? Even though the concept of pattern or system as an *explanatory* tool is now seen to be of little value, its usefulness as a tool to *describe* a number of linked processes is considerable and we can conveniently use it in the early part of this chapter.

The interaction patterns or 'systems' of the school

A starting point is to see the curriculum as one of the *interaction systems* of the school. It is one of a number of such systems that overlap and interlock with each other and which, together, constitute the large and complex pattern of interactions that we call schooling. We are all familiar with these systems; they have involved all of us in childhood and very many of us subsequently.

In addition to the curriculum system we may identify the grading or *examination system* concerned with the internal and external assessment, selection, identification and labelling of both students and teachers. There is the *teaching system* that is concerned with the division of labour involved in the curriculum, the conditions in which students and teachers interact and the approved methodologies of such interaction. There is the *control system* concerned with the establishment of behavioural norms (often through rewards and punishments that may themselves be artefacts of the system), appropriate and often ritualistic behaviours and disciplinary roles for teachers and for students such as detention masters, prefects and so on. There is also the *administrative system* concerned with such matters as attendance, health, welfare, guidance, and the organization of houses, forms, streams and other groupings.

It is quite clear that all of these systems interlock and overlap at almost every point. In particular they are all intimately interrelated with the curriculum. Alongside them there are many sub-systems of interaction, often of great importance. These may be official, such as the games system, or unofficial, such as those that operate in the playground or on the school bus. All the systems that we have considered so far may be regarded as the *micro* systems of the school and, quite clearly, the *curriculum*, concerned with the content of learning and its organization, is just such a system.

In practice the interplay of these systems may often render them indistinguishable from each other. For example, the experience of a child in a science period may, at first glance, appear to be largely determined by the content of the science curriculum. This may be particularly the case if he is following one of the 'new' curricula in which the emphases on the specifically curriculum decisions may be very much in evidence. But his experiences may be also very closely linked to the nature of the teaching system. Much could depend on whether the teaching system is 'teacher centred' or 'child centred'; the child will quickly learn that these imply important differences in the expectations surrounding his classroom behaviour. Likewise there are likely important differences in the control system that applies in different kinds of lesson; that which applies in a class working on group discovery activity is likely to be very different from that which applies to a class working on competitive individual work. There will also be important differences that spring from the method of assessment and examination that is in force and also differences that arise from the composition of the class; for example, is it one of homogeneous or mixed ability? Here the administrative system of the school is clearly important. In short the experience of any child is likely to be influenced by the interrelated operation of all these systems and, even though the curriculum is clearly a central variable, it would be quite misleading to suggest that even most of what happens within a school is determined by it. If the curriculum system were the sole or even the only major variable system in our schools then it would be far more possible to predict the behaviour of teachers and children than it is in practice.

Value and power systems

But there are other patterns within the school that we must also consider. They are at a somewhat greater level of generality than the systems we have so far considered and are less readily relateable to the day-to-day behaviour of children and teachers. These are the linked *systems of values and power* that lie at the heart of any social institution. In every school there is a *system of values* that guides the development of the other systems — it enters into decisions as to what behaviour is rewarded or punished and how; into decisions as to the ways in which pupils of different ability should be taught. Above all it enters into decisions about the knowledge and understanding offered to pupils — how it shall be defined, to which pupils shall it be offered or withheld, how it shall be evaluated — what parts shall be of high or low status? Allied to this there is the *power system* which may be glimpsed by observing by whom and at what level decisions are made, how they are executed, what methods of control are employed to ensure that they are implemented and, above all, how they are legitimated. As the value system differs in different schools so does the power system. It may be autocratic or democratic, centralized or decentralized. Of course the power system and the value system are inextricably linked and it may be necessary to treat them interdependently. Most of our terms for describing the 'regime' of a school imply 'authoritarian', 'permissive', 'rigid', 'relaxed', etc. Thus a school may be seen to be characterized by a 'repressive tolerance' with a value system that appears to tolerate a wide range of alternative behaviours yet, in its very 'toleration', creates a power structure that represses them through, perhaps, strategies of delayed or insensitive response to challenges to the established power structure.

The linked patterns of values and power are of particular importance in the study of the curriculum. Though usually forming far less a part of the everyday thinking of the classroom teacher than the other systems, they none the less rest at the very heart of the teacher's day-to-day work in the classroom. Every teacher in a classroom undertakes his work on the twin assumptions that what he is teaching is right for the children and, moreover, that he has the right to teach it. It is the value and power system of the school that supports the teacher in these views, in short, it legitimates his role. The fact that few teachers have fundamental doubts about the curriculum they are teaching, or about their right to engage in this activity, in no way diminishes this point, indeed, it reinforces it. So total is the legitimacy conferred on their activities by the value and power systems of the school that it becomes taken for granted and needs little day-to-day consideration in most schools and with most classes. The teacher who has fundamental doubts about his right to teach the curriculum is regarded at best as a crank (more readily tolerated in some subject areas than others), at worst as a deviant who 'has made a mistake' in becoming a teacher.[1]

School systems and societal systems

But when we are considering the normative and power structure of the school, we can no longer make any assumption that the school is an autonomous social institution. The norms and power system of the school must either reflect what is acceptable to the normative and power structure of society or else, in a limited number of areas that may be open to it, challenge these structures through a response that must still take them into account. Indeed, it could be argued that even one of the most advanced forms of rejection of the societal norms and power structure that we know today — the deschool or the free-school movement — is powerfully influenced in both its opportunity and its form by the normative and power structure of the society at large. The important point here is that the school has an unavoidable relationship with the wider society, that the normative and power systems of the school are not only part of the micro system of the school but also of the macro system of the whole society. Freire, the architect of a well-known curriculum designed to combat adult illiteracy in Brazil, has recently stated: 'It is impossible to think of education without discussing economic and political power . . . if you describe to me the structure of power in a society, the relations of production, I can describe to you the system of education' (1972). The importance of political power in any consideration of school systems cannot be emphasized too strongly as Evetts has noted (1973):

All educational theories are political theories. All educational arguments and ideas contain value-assumptions and include visions of utopias. Usually, educational and social arguments are inter-twined. What begins as an educational issue (selection, for example) is debated in social terms (selection is unjust because middle class children are selected and working class children are not). What is justified as an educational argument is really a social argument: social equality is the real point at issue.

There are many mechanisms that link the norms and values of society with those of the school. These include the administrative arrangements of LEAs and their officers who are responsible to elected representatives; the importance of these links to curriculum decisions is documented by Baron and Tropp (1961) who consider the role of school administrators in Britain and the United States. Further work has been done on this theme, with particular reference to the governing bodies of schools, by Baron and Howell (1974). There is also the mechanism whereby the school supplies its leavers to the occupational structure; there is the public examination system and the more diffuse but unquestionably effective mechanisms whereby public opinion on the work of students, teachers and schools may be expressed through the mass media. A more recent phenomenon is the development of public agencies for the development of the curriculum, notably the Schools Council; but also, only slightly less directly related to the curriculum, there is the work of such bodies as the National Foundation for Educational Research, the Scottish Council for Educational Research, the National Council of Educational Technology and the various research organizations, not to mention the work of various interest groups such as the Council for the Preservation of Academic Standards, the Home and School Council, the National Association of Parent Teachers, the Society for the Advancement of State Education and many others. There may also be direct governmental intervention – for example, the recent establishment in Britain of a new award – the Diploma of Higher Education – virtually by ministerial decree. There are also important diffuse interventions like the solicited and unsolicited teaching material that flows into schools from official, private, commercial and professional organizations ranging from the various ministries to the Milk Marketing Board, the Royal Society for the Protection of Birds and the manufacturers of Brooke Bond tea.

The curriculum and social control

At this stage we can see clearly that curriculum is an important part of the macro system as well as being an important part of the micro system of education. For the curriculum is one of the key areas in which the values and power system of the school and society areas come together; a key mechanism of social control over the young and over those who teach them.

We shall be exploring both curriculum control and the control through the curriculum extensively in later chapters. But even now some of the issues may readily be made clear if one considers the kind of curriculum decisions that are likely to be made explicitly or implicitly within any school in the determination of its curriculum. They include:

1 How is knowledge structured, what is the use of specialist disciplines and fields of experience or understanding, are they to be used separately or in integrated programmes?

2 What are the appropriate contents of knowledge, how much shall be taught, in what order and in what relationships?

3 What is the appropriate presentation of knowledge, how should it be taught, by which teachers, using what educational technology (methodology, texts, audio-visual aids and other equipment)?

4 What is the availability of curriculum knowledge, to whom should it be taught, at what stage and in what institutions? Should it be available universally, or even obligatory, or available only to a chosen elite?

5 What is the assessment of knowledge, how shall its acquisition be judged, and by whom, who shall be allowed to demonstrate their acquisition?

6 What are the corollaries of curriculum knowledge, notably the nature of the organizational values that curriculum is required to support?

Defining the curriculum

These questions have indicated at least some of the parameters of the curriculum; they have also illustrated some of the obvious difficulties in obtaining a satisfactory definition of the curriculum. But at this stage it may be useful to essay a simple and incomplete but brief definition and to say that the curriculum is concerned with the presentation of knowledge; and involves a pattern of learning experiences, both instrumental and expressive, designed to enable it to be received by students within the school. This pattern of learning experiences is one that responds to the societal view of the nature, distribution and availability of knowledge and is, therefore, subject to change.

Curriculum involves a number of components, including aims, content, technology (methodology), timing (order) and evaluation that spring, like curriculum itself, from the normative and power systems of society. As has already been seen, they make specific and, at times, inflexible demands on the other systems of the school, notably the teaching system but also the control system, the administrative system and the examination system. Characteristically the curriculum, whether divided into specific subject areas, disciplines, faculties, applied studies, or conceived of as integrated subject areas specific to certain age, sex or ability groups, may be expressed in a number of curriculum statements, such as a syllabus — often closely linked with a syllabus of an examination board (though attempts to change the direction of this link are being made in many schools through Mode 3 Certificate of Secondary Education Examinations and similar mechanisms, wherein efforts are made to match the examinations to the syllabus of the school rather than vice versa). Or, more generally, it may be expressed as a range of end-products or goals to be achieved by those who follow it or as a statement of aims. It may also be expressed, on occasions, as a view of learning. A characteristic of these various expressions of curriculum is that they are always somewhat larger than life; the syllabus is commonly in excess of the time available and is never fully achieved; the aims for any one subject are frequently so worded that they imply a capacity to take over almost the total curriculum of the school. One example of this is to be found in a recent statement concerning the art curriculum in the secondary school. Its contribution to the total curriculum of the school is described as follows (Schools Council Art Committee, 1975):

(a) The practical activities of an Art course make a substantial contribution to the development of personal and social skills, of aptitudes and of enthusiasms, both in terms of the growth of self-awareness as well as powers of discrimination. They achieve this because of the special satisfaction and sense of involvement which comes from the interplay between ideas, manual skills, and the disciplines and suggestions arising from the inherent qualities of the materials used.

(b) Art can provide a strong motive for the study of the human and material world; for a search for the forms of the environment, for their observation and for their recording by drawing (in its fuller sense and with a variety of media). The process of drawing itself sharpens the powers of observation and of the intellect. For example, the need to draw and record visual ideas occurs in geography as well as in art. Similarly, the keen observation and analysis of natural forms and environmental features can be a starting point for the sciences and can have an important part to play in the teaching of English. The handling of materials and tools and the sharpening of the senses that results from making things are important ways in which ideas can be developed, scientifically, technically or aesthetically.

(c) Art, like poetry, gives young people the means to communicate their thoughts and feelings. Moreover, the resulting work can be assessed by its creator, thus providing the opportunity for self-realisation and the growth of attitudes. The study of art can also bring a further understanding of ourselves and of man's aspirations and achievements.

A briefer but almost equally embracing statement is that of the National Association for the Teaching of English (1964), which reads:[2]

The teaching of English demands a permissive relationship between the school and between teachers and children if for no other reason than that of giving children opportunities of using language to express themselves honestly in a variety of situations.

The 'hidden' curriculum

By curriculum in this book we shall mean the presentation of knowledge and learning experiences in the school, though the relationship of the reality of this with the curriculum statements is clearly problematic. This reality will always include much else that is not expressed in the curriculum statements. Here we are already facing the difference between the 'official' curriculum statements and the practice of the classroom; between the formal and informal curriculum. We also need to consider 'the hidden curriculum' identified by Jackson (1968) which includes such important learning as understanding alternative orientations to the 'official' knowledge of the school, how to satisfy the teacher's requirements, how to respond to the knowledge or normative content in ways that are acceptable to one's peers as well as to one's teachers. This may include knowledge of when cheating is tacitly approved or when consistently high grades are tacitly disapproved. Response to the hidden curriculum may well be at least as important for the personal survival of the student as his response to the official curriculum. It may be of even greater importance to the teacher, for without the 'hidden curriculum' teachers may find their pupils have to 'work to rule' — as they may be unable to use mutual help before the homework is submitted (hence presenting the teacher with an impossible correction burden) or unable to 'discuss' the right answers in the science experiments.

There is, of course, much more that is 'hidden'. It could be argued that the purpose of the mathematics curriculum is not only to enable pupils to learn mathematics but also to allow some to understand that they cannot learn mathematics and to acquire a suitable respect for those who can (the teachers and the more able pupils destined for superior occupational status). If this is the case, of course, the unstreamed class or the comprehensive school may provide a more suitable arena for such learning.

The magnitude of the unofficial, informal and hidden arrangements of the curriculum is why the notion of 'purposive organized activity' so common in teacher-oriented definitions of the curriculum have been omitted in the definition offered here where we are attempting to provide a sociologically useful definition of curriculum. A sociologist must be concerned with the realities of social behaviour. If the teachers and the pupils are involved in curriculum interaction that is, in practice, defined differently from the official statements, then it is with this definition that he must concern himself, even though it may be considerably more difficult to identify than the official statements of syllabus, aims and so on.[3] (It is for similar reasons that, in their exploration of education, sociologists have generally defined the process in a way that is in no way confined to organized schooling.)

Early sociological approaches to the curriculum

Having arrived at this preliminary sociological identification of the curriculum it is now necessary to consider the range of approaches that sociologists have made. In doing so we shall begin to abandon the descriptive concept of system which is already to be seen as an oversimplification. One of the starting points of sociology was the functional analysis of education that sprang from the writings of Durkheim and which has dominated much of the work of sociology of education until recent years. For Durkheim the central function of education is socialization — methodological preparation of the young for adult life. 'Its object is to arouse and develop in the child a certain number of physical, intellectual and moral states which are demanded of him both by the political society as a whole and the special milieu for which he is specifically destined.' For Durkheim this system of education sprang from norms of the society (1956, pp. 66, 71):

> Each society considered at a given stage of development has a system of education which exercises an irresistible influence on individuals. It is idle to think that we can rear our children as we wish. There are customs to which we are bound to conform; if we flout them too

severely they take their vengeance on our children . . . there is then
in each period a prevailing type of education from which we cannot
but deviate without encountering that lively resistance which re-
strains the fancies of dissent.

All this leads, in Durkheim's view, to 'curricula' that are clearly differentiated (ibid., p. 68):

> It can be said that there are as many different kinds of education as
> there are different milieux in a given society. Is such a society
> formed of castes? Education varies from one caste to another; that
> of the patricians was not of the plebeians; that of Brahman was not
> that of the Sudra. Similarly in the Middle Ages, what a difference
> between the culture that the young page received, instructed in all
> the arts of chivalry, and that of the villein, who learned in his parish
> school a smattering of arithmetic, song and grammar! Even today do
> we not see education vary with social class or even with locality?
> That of the city is not that of the country, that of the middle class
> is not that of the worker . . . each occupation indeed constitutes a
> milieu *sui generis* which requires particular aptitudes and specialised
> knowledge, in which certain ideas, certain practices, certain modes
> of viewing things, prevail; and as the child must be prepared for the
> function that he will be called upon to fulfil, education, beyond a
> certain age, can no longer remain the same for all those to whom it
> applies.

Though it is important to recognize that Durkheim is talking about education as a whole rather than formal schooling, it would not be difficult,
building on his work, to suggest a functionalist view of the curriculum,
wherein the curriculum is seen to be serving the needs of the society to
ensure that the young receive the culture (knowledge, skills, values)
appropriate to membership of the adult society. Certainly for Durkheim, such an experience was the central task of education and, for that
part of it which takes place in the school, the role of the curriculum is
central.

It is possible to pursue a functional analysis of the curriculum in a
number of other areas than that of socialization. Following Durkheim's
lead we may consider the selective and allocative functions of the
curriculum brought about by different children following different programmes. We may go on to the equality of opportunity debate and
identify several other functions, both manifest and latent, that the curriculum 'performs'. These may include components such as anticipatory

socialization where the curriculum introduces pupils to experiences that anticipate their adult role; acceptance of differentiation where the curriculum not only makes legitimate differences between students but also through the values it embraces brings them to accept that such differences are legitimate in adult society. Here the curriculum can, as has already been noted, importantly underpin the power structure of the society; there is much evidence that it has done so in nineteenth-century and twentieth-century curricula that will be reviewed in Chapter 3. The list can continue with a number of important 'micro' functions such as the legitimation of the teaching and control systems of the school itself.

The problems of a functionalist approach

It is unnecessary to explore functionalism further to realize that the approach can be a captivating one for sociologists and its dominant role in the development of educational sociology in the 1950s and 1960s is clear. Unfortunately, it is insufficient and potentially misleading, resting on a number of questionable assumptions. It assumes that the curriculum is a unified and coherent mechanism in a consensus world. The distinction that has already been made between the official curriculum and the hidden curriculum suggests that this is fallacious; there is not only conflict there but also within the 'official' curriculum itself. Discussions in any school staffroom alert us to the fact that there is no necessary consensus concerning aims, goals, methodology or indeed any aspect of the curriculum within a school, let alone within a system.

But an even more important criticism of the functionalist approach is that it leads us to take problems as 'given', to define the behaviours and interactions, norms and goals that take place within the curriculum system in the terms of the official educator's view. Thus in the study of equality of opportunity, much of the work has taken as 'given' teachers' definitions of opportunity and achievement instead of regarding them as sociologically problematic. Young has reminded us: 'On the whole, sociologists have "taken" educators' problems, and, by not making their assumptions explicit, have necessarily taken them for granted' (1972).

We have already been guilty of this in the way we have labelled the hidden curriculum. The hidden curriculum is only hidden, if at all, to the teacher; it is clearly visible to the students — probably even more clearly visible than the official curriculum. It is impossible to consider the realities of social behaviour associated with the curriculum unless we are aware of the perceptions that the participants bring to it – their 'social constructions of reality'. Here we are concerned with the need to explore, among other things, not only the realities of behaviour in the curriculum but why it comes about that we apply such usages as we have just illustrated.

The point is important because unless the constructions of the students and of the teachers share at least some congruency, the consequences, if any, of the curriculum are likely to be different from what either side anticipates. There are many examples of dissonance in the curriculum. In the expressive subjects such as art and music, teachers are commonly concerned with 'helping children to express themselves' in such matters as music, dress, leisure and so on. Yet they are regularly heard to complain that students 'reject' the expressive activities they offer both out of school and after school. But it is not that the children are uninvolved in music, dress or leisure, rather that they have alternative perceptions of these matters that are either unrelated to or opposed to those of the teachers. It is important to remember that this does not mean that children are unable to respond to the teacher's construction of reality in these matters; indeed, most children quickly learn to perform in school in the ways approved by the teacher. Many writers have reminded us that what the child learns above all is how to give an acceptable performance. Most children are capable of and willing to give the teacher egg-crate sculpture, embroidered napkins, *avant garde* music or poetry or whatever else he desires. But giving this acceptable performance may in no way modify their construction of reality which may have its roots in areas of thought and experience not shared by the teacher. To paraphrase Bernstein (1970), if the culture of the teacher is to become part of the consciousness of the child then the culture of the child must be in the consciousness of the teacher.

The same issue may be seen at the macro level. Writing in a somewhat different context Brandis and Henderson (1970) have noted that issues such as deprivation and educational priority, with major curriculum connotations, are often seen from a viewpoint that may well be at variance from the view of social reality held by the 'deprived'. They write:

In all work concerned with comparative socialisation within a society, there is always a danger that the differences such studies reveal will be transformed into statements of 'better' or 'worse'. This is particularly the case where the groups involved are social class groups and the socialisation is into the school. Once such judgments are made, implicitly or explicitly, that one form of socialisation is 'better' than another it is but a short step to consider how we can transform the 'worse' into the 'better'. Can we make the working class as the middle class? This question is based upon the dubious premise that socialisation within contemporary middle class strata and the education we offer in the schools represents the acme of three quarters of a million years of civilisation. It equally and inevitably leads on to a view of the child as a deficit system, his parents as inadequate and their culture as deprived. The very form our research takes reinforces this view. It shows nearly always what the middle class *do* and what the working class do *not* do in relation to the middle class.

The way in which 'keeping the options' open in the comprehensive school curriculum may have reinforced the 'middle class' orientation of curriculum for a greater number of children has already been noted. Shipman (1971) notes how special courses for below average or 'Newsom Children' also reinforce this distinction by reifying it as 'the way things are'.

Alternatives to functionalist approaches

The consideration of alternative constructions of reality may be seen as a reaction to the positivism of earlier sociological approaches. Whilst this is in part true, it is important to realise that we are not substituting a total relativism in place of positivism. The sociologist is concerned with regularities and shared patterns of human behaviour. His enthusiasm to explore the individual's social construction of reality is to learn more about these regularities than before. In the area of human behaviour that surrounds the school curriculum the need is particularly great, for, as we have realized, the 'official' view is likely to be an incomplete one. Accordingly the non-positivist sociological approaches are offering us valuable assistance in reaching a fully sociological analysis of the school curriculum.

Already, we may augment our earlier definition of the curriculum in that we can now see it as a body of learning experiences responding to a societal view of knowledge that may not always be fully expressed or even fully accepted by teachers or students. The outcomes of the curriculum are likely to depend very largely on the extent to which this societal view of knowledge is shared by the school, its teachers and its students.

We shall be considering this societal view of knowledge in the subsequent chapters where we shall be exploring the difficult questions of how various curricula may be classified, how they come to be what they are in content, methodology and evaluation and how they may be selected, distributed, transmitted and evaluated. Above all we shall be concerned to explore the ways in which they may be made legitimate and the important conflicts that arise in curriculum determination.

Summary

In this chapter we have sought to set the curriculum in its context in the micro and macro social arrangements that we call schooling. Having done so we have envisaged a preliminary definition of the curriculum and the ways in which it is identified. This has been followed by a review of sociological examinations of curriculum from positivist functionalist approaches through to more recently developing non-positivist approaches. In undertaking the examination the simple descriptive concept of system has been abandoned in favour of more realistic aids to understanding reality.

3

The historical determination of the school curriculum

How is the curriculum chosen? How is one collection of knowledge selected out from an almost unlimited number of combinations? Every human group makes a selection of the knowledge it considers necessary and desirable. Moreover, such 'curricula' vary between different social situations and between different periods. Schools are no exception; each requires a selection from the vast range of knowledge available. To begin to study how such crucial decisions come about it is useful to examine the context in which they have been made up to the present time. After a résumé of some of the major historical facts three of the central areas of conflict will be discussed in detail.[1]

To write of the context of the curriculum is to write not only of the whole of education but also the whole of society. The curriculum is exposed to and in some way interacts with every aspect of the total social situation. But time and resources in the school are limited and a curriculum totally open to society is unrealistic; it would almost certainly be transitory, unmanageable and overloaded. In practice every curriculum involves a process of selection that is rigorous in nature as a result of which a selection of knowledge, understanding, values and skills are chosen for inclusion. Even though curricula may be labelled as 'open', 'flexible' or even 'child-centred', it is usually not difficult to see the results of a selection or filtering of content in what happens in the classroom. Indeed a newspaper article in the late 1960s (*Observer*, 15 September 1968) reported:

The law says nothing specific about what should be taught in schools apart from religious instruction: this has to be provided, though not necessarily by the headmaster himself, who can opt out of it on grounds of conscience. Legally he would be within his rights if he divided the curriculum between Esperanto and basketball. The education committee would object, but a man who could concoct a philosophy to support his eccentricity would be hard to shift.

Yet such curricula do not exist in practice and it is the purpose of this chapter to consider the processes of *interaction*, often partially hidden, that bring about not only a selection of curricula content but also one that is remarkably consistent and predictable. Essentially they are processes of conflict that give rise to a range of compromises, adjustments and points of equilibrium of varying degrees of stability. In all these negotiations an underlying concept is that of *power*. It may be seen as two levels – first the power to make decisions that influence the work of students and teachers and secondly the control over the power that can be achieved by students or withheld from them by determining access to high or low status curricular components and the evaluation and opportunities associated with them. Unquestionably curriculum determination is centrally concerned with both the use and the allocation of power.

At the heart of these processes in any society there are five key factors to which we have already made reference; they are:
1 the definition of what shall be regarded as knowledge, understanding, values and skills;
2 the evaluation of this knowledge – into areas of greater or lesser importance and status;
3 the principles on which such knowledge shall be distributed; to whom and at what time various kinds of knowledge shall be made available and from whom they shall be withheld;
4 the identity of the groups whose definitions prevail in these matters;
5 the legitimacy of these groups to act in these ways.
It is the final factor that is at the heart of the sociological analysis for in the last resort a curriculum exists and the power distribution is real because people believe in the knowledge it contains and the justice with which it is distributed. Indeed, it is possible, as Durkheim indicated, to regard curriculum not so much as a body of knowledge but as a 'collective representation' of a community of people.

Consideration of these factors has already suggested that the process of determining the curriculum can be regarded as a process of *social control*. As we have seen, this process of social control may most readily be identified by asking such questions as 'who is chosen to experience different curricula?' and 'what parts of such curricula are available to different children?'. Questions of this kind were first put explicitly by Warner, Havighurst and Loeb in their book *Who Shall Be Educated?* (1946) in which, through the exploration of a range of curricula and their accessibility, they showed that the differential experiences of the curriculum formed a crucial part of the social selection procedures of the United States in the 1940s. Their evocative chapter titles epitomize their approach — A Negro Girl Is Taught Her Place; An Upper-Class Boy Learns He Is Different; The Social Rise of Flora Bell.

But for many centuries the question 'who shall be educated?' was answered by reference to the distinction between the few who experienced any curriculum and the majority who did not. Formal education was generally only the experience of the children of a small and well-defined landed, political, ecclesiastical and professional elite and was of a kind suited to enable them in turn to exercise and retain the rank and status of their parents. In such a system there was little uncertainty concerning the definition of knowledge; it was defined by the traditional vocational necessities of the elite groups. Similarly its distribution was clearly prescribed. Much the same applied to the formal education available to those of humble birth. Varying widely in its availability it was predominantly provided by the church in order to provide a continuing recruitment for the priesthood — certainly it was an essential corollary to the celibacy of the Catholic priesthood. But throughout the provisions of formal education there was no ambiguity about the identity of the groups whose decision prevailed; neither was there question concerning their legitimacy. And for the vast majority who received no formal education there was no curriculum other than that of the life of the community itself.

Yet it was the elite curriculum — a curriculum based predominantly on secondary experience through books and received knowledge rather than first-hand experience — that came to characterize almost the total content of the curriculum until very recent times. In this chapter we shall be largely concerned with the social context of a curriculum originally defined by and for the elite groups of society. The sections that follow examine the process in three areas: the historical development of the curriculum; social conflict and the curriculum; and, finally, the identity of the groups who define the curriculum.

Historical development of the curriculum

The development of the content of the curriculum has been reviewed by many writers — it is a central theme in most standard histories of education.[2] The curriculum model outlined by Plato in *The Republic*, with its precise definition of knowledge and of the categories of persons who might receive it, formed an early indication of the curriculum process that we have already spoken of. Plato's content – music and gymnastics in its fullest sense – along with military training formed a persuasive model and the *trivium* and *quadrivium* of the mediaeval university – the seven liberal arts – sprang closely from it. Yet the basis of all mediaeval education was Latin. It was a vocational necessity for the church, law and medicine; it was the key to almost all learning that had survived the Dark Ages; it provided position and authority for those who mastered it.[3]

The definition of knowledge in England and Wales in the seventeenth and eighteenth centuries reflected an even greater preoccupation of the curriculum with Latin. This classical grounding came to form virtually the whole curriculum; 'useful' studies came to be associated with the usually short-lived 'dissenting academies'. But from the early years of the nineteenth century change followed the recomposition of the dominant elite which was substantially augmented by a new landed and aspirant commercial group. A new and important feature of the time, that was to prevail, was the redefinition of high-status knowledge as that which was not immediately useful in a vocation or occupation. The study of the classics now came to be seen as essentially a training of the mind and the fact that a boy could be spared from work long enough to experience this in full measure was in itself seen as a demonstration not only of the high status of the knowledge itself but also of the recipient – the mark of a 'gentleman' rather than a 'worker'. The definition, once made, tended to be self-perpetuating. Campbell (1968) notes that 'the mere fact that Latin has for centuries been taught in academically selective or high status institutions is in itself an important reason for its retention'.

The curriculum in an industrial society

The developments of the nineteenth century meant that a simple 'elite determinist' analysis of the kind we have so far explored was no longer tenable as a total explanation of the curriculum. Changes in both the roles and social composition of the higher-status groups in the industrial society led to a call for a broader (though not a vocational) education as a preparation for the wider range of public, administrative and industrial activities. At the same time the renaissance of interest in earlier forms of liberal education in the universities led, in various ways, by such fundamentally different men as Jowett and Newman, brought further reinforcement to the idea of a broader school curriculum.

The process was reinforced by the concurrent expansion in the size and recruitment of the political, professional, clerical and administrative elite in the nineteenth century, bringing a demand for increased educational provision of which the public schools were the most notable example. The staffs of the public schools, especially when led by heads who were themselves eminent scholars, such as Butler of Shrewsbury, came to be particularly responsive to the revival of Platonism in the universities and the redefinition of the public school curriculum of the time has been well reported by historians and novelists (a notable early example of the latter is Hughes's *Tom Brown's Schooldays* with its sensitive, if somewhat romantic, account of Arnold's reforms at Rugby). The changes in the public schools were strongly reinforced by the more severe examination requirements for the Honours degree introduced by Oxford and Cambridge universities.

The curricular developments in the public schools were associated with many other changes in their internal systems, in the changed methods of administration and discipline that came to be adopted and most strikingly in the new emphases on corporate life and sport. The model of the new public school curriculum came in time to be adopted increasingly by the endowed grammar schools and, after 1902, it formed a major component of the model set out by Morant for the new local education authority grammar schools. Yet the model was still one that was based largely on Latin. Thring wrote: 'Let the mind be educated in one noble subject. If this subject also embraces a wide field of knowledge so much the better. The universal consent of many ages has found such a subject in the study of Latin and Greek literature' (1867). Morant's new *Regulations for Secondary Schools* recommended, with reference to the new secondary (grammar) schools: '. . . where two languages other than English are taken, and Latin is not one of them, the Board will require to be satisfied that the omission of Latin is for the advantage of the School' (Board of Education, 1904).

The emergence of the public examination system

But the curricula changes in high-status education in the nineteenth century possibly received the greatest impetus from the gradual development of social selection based upon educational achievement. The increasing ranks of the middle classes could no longer be filled by nomination and patronage. New devices had to be found to select the additional members that were needed. The Northcote-Trevelyan report of 1864 on recruitment to the civil service was perhaps the most striking example. It introduced a new way of recruitment to the upper ranks of the civil service — a public examination system. In the home civil service, and particularly in the Indian civil service, ascriptive entry became augmented by a regularized *achievement entry*,[4] even though it quickly became clear that even in these somewhat wider patterns of recruitment the achievement tended to become open to those who had access to an appropriate education. An interesting example arose following the abolition of the purchase of military commissions and the introduction of a system of entry to Sandhurst and Woolwich in the 1870s. With considerable success, a number of public schools quickly developed 'military sides' specializing in preparation for the examinations. In short, the effect of the reforms initially was largely to restrict the entry to the civil service to the same stratum of society as before — though to a somewhat broader sector of it.

The development of the examination system proceeded apace with the widespread use of the new London University Matriculation examinations for selection for an extensive range of other callings. The process was further accelerated by the new examinations of the new professional societies, many of them achieving a widespread entry and a multiple usage.[5]

The consequences of the development of public examinations on the curriculum are central to the concern of this chapter. It was at this period that the influence of the examination on the curriculum, its content, its teaching methods and its evaluation came to be established. The requirements of the civil service examinations reflected not only the prestige of classical languages but also revived enthusiasm for Renaissance ideas in the leading grammar schools that had revived them. Their influence reinforced the move away from the pedantry of grammar schools in the eighteenth century and augmented the developments built upon the Latin and Greek curricula of the seventeenth and eighteenth centuries. By the end of the nineteenth century it became possible to identify the standard elite education as being of a predominantly 'liberal classical' nature inspired by a humanistic desire to lead pupils to an appreciation of the achievements of the classical era. In reinforcing these moves, the examination system had come, in part, to institutionalize the process of defining and evaluating curriculum knowledge. The public examinations had emerged not only as a new instrument of social selection but also as a new instrument of determination of the curriculum.

The continuing and rapid growth of this nineteenth-century invention has been one of the most notable features of twentieth-century education. Notable stages have been the establishment of the School Certificate in 1917 and the General Certificate in 1951. Since 1951 the rapid growth of O and A level Certificate examinations, followed in 1965 by the CSE examinations (Beloe Report, 1960) led to an unprecedented range of examinations requiring differentiated curricula and calling for differentiated achievement.[6]

A major pressure has arisen from the increasing numbers of occupations following the lead given by the civil service and calling for examination achievement as a prelude to entry. Reference to the 'Situations Vacant' column of any national or local newspaper gives a clear indication of the extent to which examination requirements increasingly regulate entry to a wide range of callings. For many it is important to notice that the concept of selection is the experience not of a vocational but rather of a general and liberal curriculum — an association that persists in the contemporary English school curricula since the emergence of the seventeenth-century view of non-vocational knowledge as being superior in status. (An A level in English literature may well be a more desirable asset than an A level in technical drawing in the selection of trainee executives in an engineering company.) In this context the persistent retention of liberal studies in institutions of predominantly vocational education, such as technical and further education colleges, often in face of the hostility of the student population, is notable (Cantor and Roberts, 1969).

Alternative definitions of knowledge

Yet though the 'liberal classical' curriculum predominated in the public and the grammar schools of the nineteenth century, it was not without challenge. In the latter half of the century new groups with alternative definitions of knowledge emerged. Notably these were scientists and their advocates including T. H. Huxley, H. Spencer, H. Hobhouse, J. Tyndall, M. Faraday and A. H. D. Acland, the political head of the Education Department in the 1880s, who sought a curriculum in which scientific and technical knowledge predominated. The case for the extension of knowledge was often based upon the scientific and technical education of overseas schools, notably those of Germany (Musgrave, 1967). The political significance of this 'pressure' group was marked by the Royal Commission of 1884, the establishment of the National Association for the Promotion of Technical and Secondary Education in 1887 and the passing of the Technical Instruction Act of 1889, which enabled the county councils to provide technical education. This Act and the Act of 1890 gave the councils the 'whisky money' that was used not only to build technical colleges and provide evening classes but, of particular interest, also to support scientific and technical curricula in the grammar and higher-grade elementary schools.

The ensuing growth of such new and 'alien' curricula in the grammar schools led to one of the most notable examples of conflicting definitions and evaluations of knowledge that had yet been seen in the English school curriculum. The emphases on science were firmly rejected by the majority of heads and teachers. In 1900 the Association of Assistant Masters asserted that 'numbers of the small grammar schools are at present confronted with a choice between ruin and a transformation into schools of science or technology' and went on to call for the secondary department of the Board of Education to be made 'unassailably strong, seeing that the technical can take care of itself'.

Banks (1955) in a discussion of 'Sir Robert Morant and Secondary School Curricula' notes that these feelings were not confined to the grammar school staffs and represented the views of HMIs and members of both political parties. She quotes from the report by HMI Headlam, as follows:

In the majority of schools, both those that receive grants from the Board of Education and others, I find that the nature of the literary education . . . requires the most serious attention. . . . Greek has practically disappeared . . . in many schools Latin is also disappearing. In the teaching of French there is at least hope and promise for the future. In English subjects this is not the case. The very first elements of good work are absent. It must be remembered that those who are educated in these schools are those in whose hands will rest the greater part of the local government of this country. From them come the greater number of teachers and writers for the Press. . . . While fully recognising that the natural sciences and mathematics must in very many schools have the predominant place, I submit that the neglect of and indifference to other sides of education must have a most harmful influence on the intellect and character of the nation.

The new Secondary School Regulations of 1904 initiated the administrative compromise between the liberal classical and scientific orientations and reflected not only the views of Morant but also in some degree the work of Sadler whose 'Special Reports' had revealed aspects of continental progress. It marked a further stage in the 'public' regulation of the curriculum that had been begun by the examination system. Though widely regarded as an imposition of the classical, elitist curriculum on the grammar schools, the regulations made provision for a small, contained but significant introduction of technical and science education into the secondary school curriculum; the pressures of the scientists of the 1890s had not wholly been in vain. Morant, even though widely regarded as the arch-enemy of science and technology, himself adopted a middle position: 'It has become abundantly clear that without adequate training in courses of the secondary school type, students cannot profit by the higher courses of training provided by technical institutions. . . . Hence comes the growing conviction that the best, indeed it might be said the essential preparation for higher technical education is a good general secondary school course.'[7] Yet the 'good general secondary school course' remained an essentially high-status-oriented curriculum. Nowhere has this been more in evidence than in the concept of the sixth form. As late as 1958 the Crowther Report *16–18* asked, 'How many extra children can be taken into the VI form without destroying its essential character?'[8]

The uses of high-status curricula

So far we have used the term 'high-status curriculum' to denote curricula available only to a restricted group of students. It may be useful to consider the term more clearly. Williams (1961) has suggested that there are two types of curricula that fall into this category. One is the 'liberal conservative' available to the children of the 'aristocracy and gentry', with an emphasis on character and the production of the 'educated man'. The other is the 'bourgeois' curriculum available to the merchant and professional classes, providing access to professional and other high-status occupations. The distinction is important as it indicates two different *uses* of the curriculum; it is one that has also been made by a number of other writers, notably Swift (1964). Yet the distinction is a confusing one in that it is applied to the *content* of the curriculum for, as we have seen, the high-status curriculum originated largely for its usefulness: neither the development of the liberal/classical curriculum nor that of nineteenth-century bourgeois education involved major distinction of course content. Both accepted, with little difficulty, a common model of 'the educated man' (Wilkinson, 1964). This is hardly surprising; both were concerned with a single commodity — power and its retention or achievement through the legitimation offered by an elite curriculum offering differentiation and high status.

The curriculum for the masses

So far we have considered the definition, evaluation and distribution of elite education. But the curriculum of the schools for the masses that developed after the introduction of compulsory schooling in 1870 also requires consideration. This education, for the children of the 'labouring poor', was seen to be of a fundamentally different kind, predominantly concerned with basic skills of numeracy and literacy.

Though in content almost diametrically opposite to high-status education, the mass-education curriculum may be analysed in similar ways. Unlike its counterpart it was defined and evaluated not by its consumers but by the same elite groups who defined high-status education. Its definition sprang from an appraisal of the knowledge regarded as appropriate for the new occupational roles of an industrial society. It was defined so that it did not present a challenge to the status of the knowledge on which elite curricula were based; rather it reinforced and re-emphasized the lower status of vocational and utilitarian knowledge and skills. An important characteristic of the curriculum of the new elementary schools was that it should not give the poor 'ideas above their station'; rather it should reaffirm the existing system of social stratification and ensure its acceptability and legitimation.

But the curriculum for the masses was called upon to serve far more urgent purposes than the provision of minimal skills. It was also required to facilitate social consensus. Industrialization led to the removal of whole populations from settled communities with their own established norms of social interaction; norms that were reinforced by effective sanctions of long standing. The new order led to new settlements where no such norms and sanctions existed. The breakdown in the normal ground rules of human life — matters such as respect for property, authority, religious observance and the regulation of community life — was widespread. Indeed, some industrial populations came to be characterized by their virtual immunity from the rule of law (Coleman, 1968).

An important and urgent task of the mass society was to 'establish the rule of law' and ensure its acceptance. After solutions based upon external imposition, notably through the introduction of the uniformed police, turned out to be only partially successful, the curriculum of the elementary schools (later to be joined by the higher grade schools and, in the twentieth century, by the trade and the junior technical schools) came to be the chosen instrument through which not only a selection of knowledge and skills but also of values were presented for internalization by the young. These were values that were defined as being appropriate not only for life in the mass society but also for the specific role and status for which the individual was destined.[9]

Some of the implications of this were glimpsed early. Baines (1846) suggested that 'A system of state education is a vast intellectual police force, set to watch over the young ... to prevent the intrusion of dangerous thoughts and turn their minds into safe channels.' It is important to recognize, however, that the mass curriculum with its confirmation or imposition of values on the children of the masses is similar in its nature to the elite curriculum already considered. The difference is one of distribution and of content rather than one of process. Moreover, it is a difference that springs from a definition and evaluation of knowledge that are common to both curricula. Dahrendorf (1960), echoing Durkheim, emphasizes the totality of the process:

> The individual must somehow take into himself the prescriptions of society and make them the basis of his behaviour; it is by this means that the individual and society are mediated and man is reborn as 'homo sociologicus'. Position allocation and role internalisation are complementary, and it is no accident that industrial societies have assigned primary responsibility for both processes to a single institutional order – the education system.

In practice, as Dahrendorf goes on to make clear, this meant that while the curriculum of the elite schools emphasized leadership, the curriculum of the elementary school emphasized deference, submission and even servility. Not only did the curriculum of these schools consist of low-status subjects, it also embodied fittingly low-status attitudes. Many contemporary writers have drawn attention to the persistence of these value orientations in curricula offered to 'average' or low-ability or low-stream pupils. Banks (1955) reminds her readers of the sharply differentiated curricula of the grammar (secondary) schools and the elementary schools throughout the period 1902–44.

The curriculum after 1944

The post-1944 secondary school reorganization maintained and even in-stitutionalized the longstanding distinctions between the curriculum of the grammar schools and the modern schools that came to replace the elementary schools (Ministry of Education, 1947b). The distinction was made possible by the prevailing belief in the possibility of reliable psychological differentiation of higher- and lower-ability children for whom the grammar and modern curricula respectively were suitable. By what was believed to be a convenient and predictable coincidence it was discovered that the majority of upper- and middle-class children were found to be intellectually superior and thereby able to follow an essentially 'elite', classically oriented curriculum of the modern school. Even so, the gradual development of arrangements whereby 'able' children from all social backgrounds could transfer from mass to elite education (Lowndes, 1969) did substantially increase after 1944 and was at the time sufficient to lend political acceptability to the arrangements.

As a result, the post-1944 arrangements had two major consequences for the curriculum of the secondary schools — the institutionalization of both differentiation and stratification:

1   They allowed the secondary schools to reaffirm and reinforce the differentiation in their curricula. There are many records of the development of the curricula of the post-1944 secondary schools. Stevens's account of the grammar school (1960) and Taylor's of the modern school (1963) offer good illustrations of the institutionalized divergence of curricula that developed.

2   They appeared to offer both 'scientific' and public legitimation to the differentiated distribution of knowledge into elite and mass curricula (the demise of the secondary technical schools established after the 1944 Education Act to provide a mid position between the modern and the grammar schools was even more rapid than that of the pre-1944 central and intermediate schools).

A perceptive glimpse of the modern school curriculum in the late 1950s is offered by Webb (1962):

What sort of person would the boy become who accepted the standards the teacher tries to impose? In himself he would be neat, orderly, polite and servile. With the arithmetic and English he absorbed at school, and after further training, he might become a meticulous clerk, sustained by a routine laid down by someone else, and piously accepting his station in life. Or, if he got a trade, we can see him later in life clutching a well-scrubbed lunch-tin and resentful at having to pay union dues, because the boss, being a gentleman, knows best. To grow up like this a lad has to be really cut-off from the pull of social class and gang, which luckily few of the boys at Black School are, because both of these types are becoming more and more redundant as mechanisation increases and job content decreases. For the majority who emerge from Black School, however, there is no disharmony between what the school has accustomed them to and what they find at work — tedium.

With no stretch of the imagination could Webb have been thought to have been writing of a grammar school. Even in the 1960s and 1970s the widespread use of different 'Newsom' curricula for 'Newsom' children springing from the Newsom Report (*All Our Future*, 1963) on average and below average children can be seen to perpetuate the binary curricular system.

But it is not only in the secondary schools but also in the primary schools that the binary distribution of curriculum is to be seen. It is only slightly less visible in the Ministry of Education publication *Primary Education* (1959) than it was in the official *Handbook of Suggestions* (Board of Education (1937), reprinted on a number of occasions). Both contain clear indications of differential curricula in the primary schools whilst the work of Douglas (1964) and others, has clearly charted the procedures whereby primary school pupils are identified prior to receiving different curricula. The fact that Douglas has indicated that these procedures are commonly subjective and arbitrary in no way diminishes the clarity of the distinction between the curricula and the consequences arising from them.

The curriculum and social consensus

But the learning and internalization of values in the curriculum is not only a divisive process, it may also be a unifying one. As Mead (1951) has reminded us, the curricula of the US schools have regularly sought to 'weld the nation' to bring about a sense of citizenship; of 'being American' to a population newly brought together not just from different communities but from distant nations. The symbolic representation of the nation in American schools by symbols such as the Stars and

Stripes over the teacher's desk and the President's photograph over the Principal's chair are but reminders of this central task of the curriculum in the American school system.

But one of the most notable and recurring unifying achievements of the mass curricula has been their success in bringing about common *acceptance* of the very curricular differences we have discussed so far. They have succeeded, for the most part, in bringing the young to an acceptance of the rightness of a superior-status curriculum for others — and also an acceptance of the superior life-chances of those who receive it. As we have already suggested in the previous chapter, it is not too cynical a view to suggest that one of the features of mass curricula may be seen as the provision of experiences which emphasize the student's *in*capacity and thereby further his acceptance of the legitimacy of different curricula for 'those who can'. Indeed his whole experience of the curriculum may be defined as bringing a shared acceptance of social differences — strongly reinforced by the administrative control systems of the school that legitimate differences in rank and status between individual children whilst still at school.

Cultural and social reproduction

This account of the context of curriculum definition, evaluation and distribution has been largely focused on developments in Britain. Whilst curricula in all school systems reflect the differences in the social structure of the societies in which they operate there are fundamental differences in the manner and in the effectiveness with which the structure may be reproduced or sustained by the curriculum. The development of the school curriculum in England and Wales is, to use Smith's (1971) terms, characterized by considerable lateral autonomy and low vertical integration and centralization. This contrasts with the development of curriculum in France which, with its Napoleonic system of central administration, often appears to have almost diametrically opposite characteristics. Yet there are sufficient similarities in the total processes of the two systems to make the analysis that Bourdieu (1971) has undertaken of the French system valuable in illuminating further features of the situation in Britain.

Bourdieu defines the historical process of socialization through education as one of *reproduction*. But he distinguishes between two kinds of reproduction — *cultural reproduction* and *social reproduction*. Cultural reproduction is mainly transmitted through the life style of the family and the experiences it leads to, notably in the home but also in the school. Social reproduction, on the other hand, is the transmission of social capital, the social and economic characteristics of the family and its material and political structure. Bourdieu sees the curriculum as predominantly an instrument of cultural rather than social reproduction. He also regards cultural reproduction as being contained within and therefore but a part of social reproduction. Such a model, which Bourdieu supports by considerable research evidence, is compatible with the developments in Britain that have been considered here where curriculum has been largely identified as a dependent variable contained within the political and economic structure (social reproduction) but linked with home and family (cultural reproduction). Interestingly, Bourdieu's analysis places little emphasis on the role of the curriculum as an instrument of social selection, in contrast to the ambitious expectations of many British educators. Yet British experience since the implementation of the Northcote-Trevelyan report, confirmed by recent research by Little and Westergaard (1964) and by Lee (1968), indicates that there has been little evidence of any major element of social mobility through educational achievement. This is not to say that the curriculum does not play an important, even inescapable role in cultural and social reproduction; rather that it is a legitimating one rather than a causal one. Cultural and social selection is reinforced rather than gained through the curriculum — though increasingly it is a reinforcement that cannot readily be dispensed with in most sections of modern inductional societies.

Key areas of social conflict over the curriculum

The résumé of the development of the curriculum to 1960 has clearly indicated that the determination of the curriculum, contrary to many expectations, is not a process of *consensual interaction* that gives rise to a simple *reproduction and maintenance* of the social structure. The reality of the conflict over curricula has already been glimpsed clearly in our analysis — notably in the discussion of the scientific challenge to the classical curriculum in the 1890s and the 'truce position' achieved by Sadler, Morant and others. We may now identify the curriculum conflict more closely by examining three main forms that have characterized curriculum decisions in the period under review. They are the conflict concerning *distribution*, the conflict concerning *evaluation* and the conflict concerning curriculum *definition* itself.

Conflict over distribution

The first, the *conflict over distribution*, has dominated much of the sociological analysis of education to date. In popular terms the conflict has been seen to be one of the attempts by and for schools and pupils associated with low-status sectors of the curriculum to achieve access to the higher-status areas. This is one of the themes of works such as Lowndes's *Silent Social Revolution* (1969), where the history of the curriculum is, in part, presented in terms of the slowly increasing entry of able elementary school pupils to the liberal classical curriculum of the grammar schools.[10] In this analysis significance again attaches to the Education Act of 1902 when the availability of the grammar-type curricula was increased through the opening of the new secondary schools in a reorganization that continued, unevenly, from 1902 until 1944. As Silver (1973) has shown, it is the conflict over distribution that has also characterized much sociological research springing from the 'political arithmetic' studies of the 1930s through to the major work on social mobility in the 1950s. Yet these studies, as with most others, involve an analysis of the conflict that is based upon an acceptance of elite forms of education as being at least more generally appropriate if not even generally desirable for all children. The research and the debate that sprang from it, for the most part, regarded only the distribution rather than the evaluation or the definition of knowledge as problematic.

Most of the major conflicts over curriculum have followed this restricted form. The 'Cockerton Judgment' of 1900 followed the attempts by the London School Board to extend the elementary curriculum in the higher-grade classes ('higher tops') of the elementary school so that it incorporated aspects of the classical liberal curriculum of the grammar schools – an attempt that was ruled to be illegal. The conflict over secondary education since 1944 has been, for the most part, a conflict of a somewhat similar nature. The implementation of the 1944 Education Act effectively excluded the pupils of the secondary modern schools from the General Certificate Examinations on the ground that their curricula, being different and shorter, made such examinations inappropriate. The efforts made by a number of secondary modern schools to challenge this restriction and to provide extended and examination courses has been documented by Taylor (1963). It is the same conflict that has dominated many of the arguments about the introduction of comprehensive education in the 1960s.

One of the major reasons why it was possible for the conflict over the curriculum to be largely contained on the distribution issue sprang from the success of psychologists in bringing about an acceptance of the existence of objective and measurable human differences (to which attention has already been given). This made it possible to redefine the distribution of access to high-status and low-status curricula as no longer being one between high-status people and low-status people but rather between able and less-able people. Not only did this have the effect of leaving the definition of knowledge and its evaluation untouched but also it largely contained the debate about distribution within a limited and manageable form in which the key question was seen to be 'How may *able* children get their chance regardless of their background?'.

The way in which the conflict has been 'managed' in this way is one of the more remarkable features of the development of curriculum in England and Wales. As we have already noticed it has been a 'management' that has left also the definition and evaluation of knowledge largely untouched and, until the past decades, led to a consensus on these matters that has led to largely static curricula in the secondary schools and, to a somewhat lesser extent, in the primary schools too.

Conflict over evaluation

The second area of conflict is that over the evaluation of the curriculum. Here the argument focuses on the attempts to bring about the redefinition and re-evaluation of low-status components of the curriculum. The effort to give higher status to areas such as vocational and technical studies, to applied subjects like book-keeping or typewriting, to 'non-academic' studies like art and craft, or even to the curricula of the central school or the secondary modern school, have been the basis for a continuing but low-profile conflict during the past century.

Unlike the distribution debate, the evaluation debate has been largely an 'inside' professional debate, conducted within the schools and colleges, within the professional associations such as the Assistant Masters Association and the National Union of Teachers and most notably within the specialist organizations such as the National Association for Teaching of English and the National Society of Art Education.

Indeed the history of some of the professional subject associations is predominantly the history of the struggle to enhance the evaluation of the subject in question – for example, the development of the Institute of Handicraft Teachers, later the Institute of Craft Education. Hanson has described the similar history of the Society of Art Masters, later the National Society of Art Education (1971). His account of the affairs of the Society of Art Masters at the turn of the century illustrates the complex paths trodden by many of the 'lower-status' professional groups in their pursuit of the re-evaluation of their area of the curriculum:

> The Society was aided in its bid to attract members when it obtained the right to award academic dress. Originally, certification was in the hands of the Department of Science and Art and later the Board of Education, but the Council of the Society of Art Masters was anxious that extra symbols of status and professional respectability should be obtained — namely academic dress and initials to place after one's name. It was decided that the Fellowship of the Society (FSAM) should be awarded to members who produced evidence of their artistic competence and ability to pay a fee. Later the ability to prepare a dissertation upon an acceptable theme was made compulsory. In 1907, when the project was introduced, nine Fellowships were granted, but several Council members had few illusions about the worth of the award. A Mr Fisher stated 'We know the initials are a sham, but they carry weight with non-intellectual bodies' (he was referring to LEAs and governing bodies).

Perhaps the major achievement in the re-evaluation debate was the gradual incorporation of science into the grammar school curriculum following the events of the 1890s. Apart from this, until the past decade, only modest success has been achieved by the advocates of re-evaluation. New subjects have been successfully introduced into the school curricula but almost always these were sub-divisions or modifications of existing high-status subjects, such as English literature, geography and history, and almost always such subjects had to preserve the form and manner of the original high-status subjects from which they sprang. The social sciences, though belatedly succeeding in the universities where they were able to adopt a pure science model (Kuhn, 1970), made only slight progress in the schools with the possible exception of economics which was able to gain an *entrée* in the slightly more flexible area of the grammar school sixth form curriculum. But the existing low-status subjects such as handicraft, art and craft and home economics (domestic science), despite strenuous efforts to adopt high-status forms of scholarship and written examinations, tended to remain unchanged. Attempts to introduce new subjects have been met by a largely inescapable demand to identify themselves with existing subjects and their evaluation. Thus the emergent subject of 'technology', having links with both the sciences and with the craft subjects, has found itself in a characteristic dilemma whereby the need to achieve status and recognition have led its advocates increasingly to emphasize its science connections. Yet often the enthusiasm to embrace it in the schools has sprung predominantly from the low-status craft teachers who, with obvious reasons, have been anxious to achieve the enhanced status that work in this field may bring them. In general the relative failure of the various advocates of curriculum re-evaluation to bring about significant changes in evaluation has largely been a consequence of their failure to achieve any substantial redefinition of high-status knowledge.[11] Only in the past ten years has the concept of curriculum development and research made new initiatives in curriculum re-evaluation more feasible; this will be discussed in the chapter on curriculum development since 1960 (though the argument will be offered that, even in innovatory conditions, curriculum re-evaluation is still likely to be more apparent than real).

Conflict over the definition of curriculum knowledge

The third and most fundamental conflict is over the central issue of the definition of knowledge. For the reasons already considered this form of conflict has so far received relatively little attention. The only consistent professional attention has sprung from the progressive school movement whose members have regularly attempted to redefine knowledge using criteria other than those of the liberal/classical tradition (Stewart, 1972). Until recently the work of the progressive movement was, for the most part, encapsulated in the independent progressive schools and only infrequently responded to by the mass of state schools or even by other independent schools. More recently, however, their influence on the state system, notably in the primary schools, has become somewhat greater, a development that will be discussed more fully in the following chapter.

Outside the professional debate, the development of working-class education provided an equally consistent challenge to high-status definitions of knowledge. Hobsbawm, in his *Labour Aristocracy* (1956), describes a nineteenth-century labouring elite that early began to develop an alternative definition of knowledge that was at variance to the classical model. Williams, in his *Long Revolution* (1961), draws attention to the challenge to the nineteenth-century definition of knowledge offered not so much by the curricula of working-class institutions such as the Mechanics' Institutes with their predominantly technical curricula, but rather through the indirect enhancement of class consciousness and identity that they helped to foster — a consciousness that was slowly embodied in a political form, often with the aid of the Workers' Educational Association and the University Extension Classes and many local organizations such as the Sunday morning classes of many industrial areas.[12]

In the twentieth century the continuing efforts of some of the teachers and administrators working in the elementary schools, the trade schools and the junior technical schools to achieve a distinctive and recognized sector of knowledge enjoying the same high station as the academic grammar school has already been mentioned. There was a recurring political accompaniment to the efforts in the debates of both the Labour Party and the Independent Labour Party, the trade unions and affiliated organizations where sporadic efforts were made, usually by individuals, to redefine the cultural traditions and knowledge of the working classes. Early in the century McTavish (1916) expressed the view of the Labour Party directly (p. 5):

> Labour wants from Education health and full development for the body, knowledge and truth for the mind, fineness for the feelings, goodwill towards its kind, and, coupled with this liberal education, such a training as will make its members efficient, self supporting citizens of a free self-governing community.

McTavish's views were reiterated some twenty years later by Cole (1935, p. 252):

> A much clearer approach to real equality of education and culture is among the most important of all socialist objectives. We have to rid our minds of the notion that a low standard of intellectual or cultural attainment is the natural accompaniment of manual or routine clerical labour. It is as possible for a factory operative or a miner to possess and enjoy the highest culture and education as it is for a highly placed civil servant and professional man.

Yet as Bourne (1976) has clearly shown, the enthusiasm for discussion on education by the British left wing in the 1920s and 1930s was slight and such debate as took place was largely focused on the conflict over distribution under the persistent leadership of Tawney (1922) — a preoccupation that continued at least into the early 1960s.

As with the debate on the evaluation of curriculum knowledge, so with the debate on the redefinition of curriculum knowledge — the active phase in the schools scarcely began in Britain until the 1960s when the impact of the alternative definitions offered by the progressive schools and other minority groups was gradually augmented by teachers, politicians, parents and students who came to believe that, for possibly the first time, the opportunity to change the fundamental definitions of the curriculum was within their grasp. The rapid development of curriculum innovation and experiment, the establishment of teachers' centres and teachers' workshops, of bodies ranging from the Schools Council to the Goldsmiths' Curriculum Laboratory, the emergence of curriculum studies as an apparently legitimate area of study in the colleges and departments of education; all these and much more were evidence of the enthusiasm for this new aspiration. Again it will be convenient to consider this upsurge of activity in the chapter on curriculum development and decision making since 1960.

The institutionalization of curriculum conflict

In this chapter and subsequently it is necessary to make reference to a phenomenon that has come to characterize curriculum particularly in recent years — the institutionalization of public conflict in the curriculum. In the historical period with which this chapter has been mainly concerned, the conflict has largely been a latent one. Yet the gradual emergence and public statement of alternative evaluation, distributions and definitions has given rise to the public defence of the longstanding distribution, evaluation and definitions in such forms as the *Black Papers* (1968–75), the publication of the Campaign for the Preservation of Educational Standards (Dyson, 1972) and similar movements. In these there is, for the first time, an attempt to make explicit the previously implicit argument in favour of the liberal classical curriculum. The circumstances leading to this set of public statements and the counter-statements in the form of publications such as *Education for Democracy* (Rubinstein and Stoneman (eds), 1970) and those of many writers on the radical alternative in curriculum, again forms the subject of subsequent chapters which take on the task of examining the continuing development of the curriculum.

It is essential at this stage, however, not to see these areas of conflict over the definition, evaluation and distribution of knowledge in the curriculum as being a conflict simply between elitism or egalitarianism, between 'open' or 'closed' curricula, or between liberal and vocational contents. The fundamental conflicts are over the identity and legitimacy of the rival contenders for membership of the groups who define, evaluate and distribute knowledge and the power these confer.

Vaughan and Archer (1971) in an analysis of social conflict and educational change in England and France from 1789 to 1898 developed a theory of ideological conflict in education that is seen to take place between *assertive* and *dominant* groups. Their discussion of the implementation of educational goals has considerable relevance for the discussion of curriculum in this volume even though the areas of conflict often took place in a markedly less structured and systematic context than in the second half of the twentieth century. The writers are particularly concerned with the *ideology* of the dominant and assertive groups as the following quotation makes clear — a quotation that also illuminates the application of their theory to the interactions wherein educational goals, including curriculum goals, are implemented:

> Thus ideology is not only a component of successful domination and assertion, but also defines the means by which educational goals can be implemented. Therefore it not only functions as a source of legitimation for domination and assertion, but also a wider educational philosophy for the dominant and assertive group. Bearing these points in mind, the ideology adopted by either type of group can be said to serve three distinct purposes — those of legitimation, negation and specification. While each of these may not be stressed to the same degree, they must be considered related to one another within a given educational ideology.

> As has been seen, both the dominant and assertive groups must seek to legitimate their position to their followers as well as to a wider audience. This involves an appeal to certain principles consonant with the interests the group represents, but not derived automatically from them.

> Secondly, the same principles must be extended to constitute a negation of the sources of legitimation advanced by other groups. With an assertive group this happens immediately, since the claims of domination must be undermined before challenge is possible. It is because of this that assertive groups in their earliest stages may concentrate almost exclusively upon negation, that is upon unmasking

or condemning the interest concealed by the ideology of the dominant group. However, a group whose domination has been unopposed over a long period may only begin to develop this negative function in proportion to the attacks launched at it. This is why the typical response of a well-established dominant group to new assertion is an immediate reformulation of its ideology, intended to strengthen its source of legitimation by extending it to negate the claims of other groups. Thirdly, a specification of the blueprint to be implemented within educational establishments, their goals, curricula and intake, must be derived from the same ideological principles.

Though written with reference to the period 1789–1898 it is not difficult to relate Vaughan and Archer's analysis to the more recent conflicts about the curriculum reviewed in this chapter between the classical traditionalists and the radical alternative advocates. Of particular interest is the compatibility between their concept of non-rational shared ideologies and the phenomenological view of knowledge definition as a shared and relativist construction of reality. There is indeed a particularly close link between Vaughan and Archer's opposed dominant and assertive ideologies and the contemporary dialectic between those who hold that knowledge is 'given' and those who hold that it is no more than an artefact constructed by man.

Who defines knowledge?

Our discussion of the groups who define knowledge, its evaluation and distribution, brings us inescapably to the point where we should attempt to identify the *composition* of these groups.

In earlier periods the identification of individual personnel is occasionally possible. Webster, in an article on the scholastic curriculum from 1640 to 1660 (1971), is able to identify by name most of the key figures in the relevant elite groups and in doing so offers an illuminating picture of the changing definition of the curriculum of the time. Vaughan and Archer in their somewhat more recent period are also able to go some way to a similar identification of personnel; in their exploration of assertive ideology at the time of the Chartist movement they are able to write (1971, p. 90):

As the main political philosopher contributing to the People's Charter Lovett was able to assert simultaneously universal franchise and general schooling. As a political reformer, he has to assign priorities: either the granting of the franchise could be viewed as a pre-requisite of universal instruction, or alternatively mass education could be presented as a necessary condition of political participation. This choice would inevitably influence both political and educational working-class activities.

Discussion of the role of the church may also be illuminated with the names of individuals and groups. Newman and Arnold stand out not only for their importance as leaders of competing groups within the church, but also for their subsequent educational influence. Hurt (1970) indicates how Lancaster and Bell, the leading Nonconformist and Anglican advocates of the monitorial system, directly influenced not only curriculum but also methodology. He cites Bell's instruction 'the words, whatever be the number of syllables of which they consist, are read in the first instance, syllable by syllable, as if they were monosyllables, thus . . . mis-re-pre-sen-ta-ti-on . . .'.

The educational pressure group

It is, however, necessary to consider an increasingly wide range of personnel as educational arrangements become both more complex and more systematized. By the mid-nineteenth century the *education pressure group* had emerged as an effective force. Their roots sprang from organizations such as the Birmingham Lunar and Manchester Philosophical Societies. Predominantly middle-class entrepreneurial in composition, they had been, in the past, excluded through religion from the endowed schools and through social class from political participation until 1832. Groups such as these, in search of a secular and scientific curriculum, played a particularly important part in the establishment of progressive experimental schools (Adamson, 1964):

> One consequence of the existence of these privately established institutions was the foundation of a curriculum which first found a place for modern studies, and in the end made English grammar and history, elementary mathematics, geography, drawing and a branch of science (usually chemistry) the staple courses of study in schools of their type.[13] They were not fettered by ancient statutes or traditional methods of teaching; but they were very susceptible to the opinions which ruled beyond the school walls, especially as these were held by parents. During the nineteenth century the conception of what constituted secondary instruction underwent a profound

change; so far as professional theory and practice influenced the change, it was due not to any Public School or Public School master but to the enterprise of the private schools.

An early group of influential decision makers were the members of the X Group who formed one of the first examples of the pressure group as we now know it in education. Brock in his 'Prologue to Heurism' (1971) writes of this group:

> The most important of these elements was a distinctive and deliberate propaganda movement, or pressure group, which advocated laboratory teaching from the 1840s onwards. The epicentre of this movement was a group of nine men who met and dined regularly each month in London and who called themselves the X-Club. (Shades of the eighteenth-century Lunar Society who had also been intensely interested in practical scientific education!) Recent studies in the sociology of Victorian science by Walter Cannon and Roy MacLeod have demonstrated the significance of 'networks' of scientists like the X. Victorian scientific networks shaped and directed the course of scientific activity through the public fronts of scientific societies, the British Association for the Advancement of Science, the universities and other scientific institutions. The X, in particular, were noticeably successful in bringing the issue of science education before these institutions and government itself.

The pressure group is now, of course, a major *entrée* to the process of knowledge definition. They are legion and range from major organizations such as the Confederation of British Industry and the Trades Union Congress through to a range of denominational, industrial and other groups with varying degrees of influence. These not only attempt to influence established groups of decision makers — government, church, local authorities and the various professional associations — but also the schools and even their pupils directly. Thus in a single week schools may receive 'teaching packs' from bodies such as the Milk Marketing Board, the British Iron and Steel Federation, the Royal Society for the Protection of Birds, memoranda from the Family Planning Association on contraception, literature from the Campaign for Educational Standards and from the Society to Oppose Corporal Punishment. To the extent that this information is not only received but also frequently used, then it must be regarded as a component of the process of knowledge definition.

Educational publishers have for long played an indirect but powerful role in the process of curriculum determination. Their influence has, like that of most others, been exercised positively and negatively. The positive influence has been through the selection of curriculum materials to be available to schools or even to publish encyclopaedic guides to the curriculum such as, for example, the six-volume *Book of School Handwork* published between 1910 and 1914, 'designed to serve every need of the teacher of handwork in the elementary schools'. But the influence has not always been positive; the availability and pricing of books, not to mention their very permanency, has also acted as a powerful barrier or at least disincentive to curriculum change; a disincentive likely to be reinforced in view of economic problems of both schools and publishers in the late 1970s. Certainly educational publishers have been able to play a crucial, if not always an innovative, role in the definition of curriculum knowledge as well as its availability. Since the 1960s the wider range of media currently being produced by publishers show signs of being likely to extend this degree of influence; the links between commercial publishers and the Schools Council through the Schools Council Publishing Company are of particular interest (Bell, 1975).

There are also the specialist agencies and *cadres* within the education service itself. One of the most notable and influential is the *Inspectorate* (HMI) which, beginning with powerful executive and supervisory powers, has, through greatly increasing emphasis on advisory roles and the monitoring of innovation, played an unobtrusive but central part in curriculum affairs throughout the period under review. There is the Schools Council and the range of emergent 'curriculum development agencies'. There are the professional associations of which mention has already been made, particularly those concerned with specialist subject areas of knowledge. There are the teachers who, both collectively and individually, have come increasingly to aspire to play an active part in the definition of knowledge in the curriculum. There are also the students who, even in the 1950s, in school systems characterized by open choices in matters such as 'staying-on' and option courses, had come to exercise themselves, through their decisions, a part in distributing, evaluating and determining the curriculum. All of these will be discussed in fuller detail in subsequent chapters.

Employers, parents and local communities also express their views on the curriculum in many ways. This may be either directly through their willingness or unwillingness to employ pupils who have received different kinds of curriculum, through their desire to pay fees for alternative curricula in independent schools, or through their membership of pressure groups. All can be seen to have 'shared' in the decisions on the distribu-tion, evaluation and definition of knowledge. When we re-ask the ques-tion 'Who defines knowledge?' it appears that the range of personnel who undertake this task has broadened from being a closely knit elite, in which the individual members may even be identified personally, to comprising virtually the whole community in its various groupings and areas of influ-ence. Such a change appears to be compatible with what Durkheim saw as a change from a mechanical society to an organic society; a change from a society in which roles and curricula were *prescribed* and into which the in-dividual fitted to a society in which the roles and curricula were *achieved*, in a way that allows the individual himself to develop his role.

Yet it is important to remember the incompleteness of moves to the 'organic' determination of the curriculum. There are two major reserva-tions. Earlier, in the discussion of conflict over the curriculum, it was suggested that conflict had been largely restricted to the argument over the distribution of knowledge and had been minimal over the issues of the determination and evaluation of knowledge. It follows that effec-tive participation in curriculum decision making has also been largely restricted to decisions about distribution – a conclusion that appears to be valid when the content and evaluation of the knowledge in the exist-ing curricula in most schools is examined. Even in schools that are characterized by 'democratic' decision making the prevalence of long-standing subjects and traditional status rankings is notable. There are of course many internal, structural and organizational factors that may contribute to this state of affairs, as Bernstein has noted (1971).

A more fundamental reservation to the democratization thesis springs from an examination of the areas in which curriculum decision making is made available to a wide population. There are considerable indications to suggest that the critical decisions on the high-status curri-culum areas are still 'reserved'; that much of the extended decision making that is effectively available to parents, students and even inno-vatory bodies such as the Schools Council is often confined to low-status areas of knowledge, and its evaluation and distribution (Young, 1972). These indications will form an important topic of discussion in subse-quent chapters. None the less, the *manifest* involvement of personnel in curriculum decision making may be indicated in Figure 1 which attempts to bring together several of the many historical strands of the present chapter – the move from a 'dominant' to an 'assertive' ideology and that from one of apparent consensus to one of institutionalized conflict.

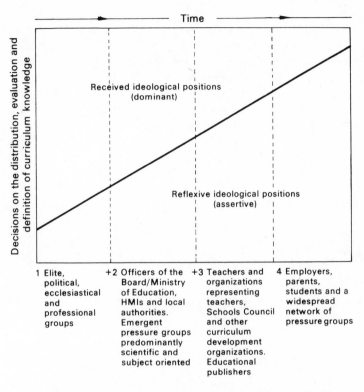

Participant groups incremental (e.g. 1-2, 3 and 4 are involved in the right-hand sector)

Figure 1

The figure emphasizes the incremental nature of the range of groups involved in knowledge determination and also makes clear that it is the increasing size of the challenge to the dominant or received ideologies rather than the overthrow of such ideologies that is being considered. It is also important to emphasize, however, that conflict is only occasionally manifest; far more it is the latent conflict over knowledge that brings about manifest changes to the curriculum. A major forum for such conflict is within the school — in the staffroom, the classroom and in the playroom. It is to these areas that we shall turn in subsequent chapters.

Summary

In an attempt to explore the factors underlying the choice of curriculum, critical areas of decision making up to 1960 have been reviewed. Following this review attention has been given to three central areas of conflict — over distribution, evaluation and definition. After an attempt to identify the participants in curriculum decision making, the chapter concludes with a diagrammatical portrayal of some of the major themes of the chapter.

4

Contemporary ideological perspectives on the curriculum

In the review of developments to 1960 we have explored the continuing conflict over the distribution, evaluation and definition of the curriculum and some of the strategies used by those who participate in the conflict. A consequence of the conflict has been the increasing complexity and variety of curriculum experienced by students in the schools. Yet the complexities of the curriculum up to 1960 are as nothing compared to the diversity that has followed. A glance at the weekly schedule of a 14-year-old student in a comprehensive school may reveal a list that not only includes such ingredients as mathematics, English, history and geography but also experiences labelled as leisure activities, social studies, design education, integrated studies, community projects, minority time and much else. How may the multitude of experiences that are subsumed within the school timetable be examined in a way that provides a useful basis for a sociological analysis?[1]

One of the keys to the analysis of the curriculum is to find ways in which this bewildering range may be conceptualized. The study of curriculum abounds with labels — traditional and progressive; child-centred and teacher-centred; open and closed — almost every curriculum theorist adopts his own new labels to arrive at his personal definition of curriculum reality. Books and even series of books abound in which the overlapping ranges of activities that may be practised under the various labels of the timetable are explored and documented. Many such studies often provide no more than arguments that can be used by the participants in the particular subject area under review to reinforce their present practices and identity. To explore the sociology of the curriculum we must, for the moment, defer the pleasure of discussing the day-to-day practice of the contemporary curriculum until we have armed ourselves with more fundamental conceptual bases that take account of the reasons why things are taught as well as their methodology

51

and their anticipated consequences. To take the most direct route to the core areas of sociological interest it is necessary to consider the ideological perspectives underlying curriculum and the important implications for the exercise of power that spring from them.[2]

Two ideological models of curriculum

In order to achieve these this chapter is built around the juxtaposition of two ideological models of curriculum. We shall call these two models the *received perspective* and the *reflexive perspective*. Like all other models these names are as oversimplified and as arbitrary as their composition. The excuse for their use lies in their capacity to initiate the understanding of complex issues. Like crutches they can later be discarded. In part the models spring from the dominant and assertive perspectives of Vaughan and Archer (1971) discussed in the last chapter. But the received perspective is not just a dominant one. It is one in which curriculum knowledge, like other components of the knowledge system in the social order, is accepted as a received body of understanding that is 'given', even ascribed, and is predominantly non-negotiable. Essentially it is non-dialectic and consensual. Similarly the reflexive perspective is more than just an assertive one. It is one in which curriculum knowledge, like the components of the knowledge system, is seen to be negotiable; in which content may be legitimately criticized and argued or new curricula devised. Essentially it is dialectic and manifestly subject to political and other influence; a construction of those who participate in its determination. Together the two perspectives represent polar views on the nature of social control and the distribution of power in society; curriculum being but one component of the interrelated arrangements for order in the social system.

After outlining the two perspectives we shall consider the ways in which they have been articulated in the discussion of curriculum and then explore the ways in which they have been justified and 'legitimized'. In our consideration of the justification of the received perspective we shall rely heavily on the work of the philosophers and psychologists; in considering the justification of the reflexive perspective we shall rely on the work of sociologists. But though this fairly represents the distribution of the current literature it is important to remember that much of the work of philosophers and psychologists can be seen to have powerful reflexive characteristics and conversely many sociologists, even those who proclaim their adherence to the reflexive perspective, have unmistakably received orientations. No philosopher, psychologist, sociologist or perspective has a monopoly on objectivity, interpretation or truth. There is no 'right' theory that will explain the dynamic nature of the curricula or of knowledge itself.

The received perspective

The history of the curriculum of the previous chapter has provided some clues to the nature of received perspective. Some of the most recurring phrases of the literature are those that speak of such things as 'the essential nature of subjects' and 'the fundamental understandings' of certain areas of the curriculum. There is a recurring desire to confer legitimacy and even permanence on the contents of almost any curriculum. 'Subjects' become 'disciplines' and in so doing achieve something very close to immortality. Disciplines that, over the years, are commonly taught in proximity become faculties – the arts, the sciences and more recently the social sciences – and in so doing their relationship becomes almost sacred. Links between areas of knowledge become reified under titles such as 'integrated studies'. Some areas of the curriculum take on the label 'pure' and in so doing claim a legitimacy usually considered to be greater than the 'applied' legitimacy of other subjects. Others may become designated as 'higher' or 'advanced' and only be available to those in the higher reaches of the education system – possibly even at post-doctoral level or else restricted to those who are licensed or qualified in some way.

In its fundamentals the perspective is received by the teacher and by his pupils as part of the given order. Associated with it in the school are established standards, norms of behaviour, rituals and hierarchical social divisions. Beyond the school it is part of an established social order in which the nature and distribution not only of knowledge but also of power is seen to be given and, for the most part, unchanging.

The reflexive perspective

Set against the reflexive perspective we can see its alternative – that curriculum is an artefact; constructed by teachers and others responsible for determining the experience of students. (In some situations the students themselves may be seen to take part in this construction.) Corroboration of such a view may spring from the often striking differences that seem to take place in the definition of important knowledge in the various subjects of the school curriculum. To many adults new mathematics seems to be different in nature from the mathematics of their own childhood (Watson, 1976). The revolution currently taking place in geography, where the emphases on regionalism are replaced by quantified accounts of location and human usage of resources, is equally notable (Boden, 1976). In literature 'new writers' become incorporated into the curriculum, often fundamentally opposed in style and syntax to the former 'greats' they replace. And the emergence of new subject areas from technology through to film studies also casts doubt on the ultimacy of curriculum knowledge.

It is important to emphasize that, as in reality, no curriculum can be absolute, so too it cannot be wholly relative, springing from nothing more than the way in which men choose to determine it. Certainly the reflexive perspective does not imply that men have regularly and consciously exercised such determination; indeed the advocates of this perspective agree that both teachers and students have played little part in the definition of curriculum (and by implication that they could and should play a greater part). But the perspective does suggest that important parts of the definition, distribution and evaluation of curriculum knowledge are the consequences of human choices and that important sociological consequences flow from such choices.

The articulation of the perspectives

Both perspectives are of long standing; they were visible throughout the discussion of culture with which the book began and remained visible throughout the historical discussion that followed where it was suggested that what is new in the past decade has been the clearer and more coherent articulation of both. The articulation of the received perspective has been seen to be, in part, a reaction to the emergence of the 'progressive' viewpoint in curriculum where the longstanding view of the curriculum has been steadily 'eroded' by strategies of child-centred education, flexible curricula, spontaneous activities and much else; an erosion that appears to have taken place with increasing speed since the 1960s. The codification of the received perspective has been most visibly undertaken in the four separate volumes of *Black Papers* that have appeared in the period 1968 to 1975: publications that would have been superfluous during the long decades when belief in the self-evidence of the view they represent was so widespread that it only needed occasional reinforcement on school speech days and similar occasions.

The National Council for the Preservation of Educational Standards was formed to affirm essentially 'received' orientations to the school curriculum. One of its sponsors (Dyson, 1972) has expressed some of the fundamental tenets:

> In place of rich and tried styles of human and social living we have a restless quest for novelty as an end in itself. Great ideas, great schools and institutions are recklessly bulldozed, before there is anything clear or coherent to put in their place. Or worse they are replaced by structures attuned to their individual creators or to the guessed needs of the moment ('social relevance'), and made wholly subservient to fashion and whim. The most basic insight of all civilisation is violated — that freedom, happiness, fulfilment exist only in a framework of law and structure, and in continuing and fruitful tension between present and past. By the same token structure is the essence of all reputable and efficient institutions which cannot be always and restlessly in charge. A school exists to pass on numeracy and literacy, civilised manners and morals, skills and achievements; how can it do this if its purpose is challenged or lost?

The articulation of the reflexive ideology also has a long history. As we saw in the previous chapter, this has its roots in the advocacy of alternative curricula throughout the nineteenth and early twentieth centuries. Since the early 1960s the constructed view has been increasingly advocated by the progressive educators with programmes of curriculum development and innovation. An early general statement of such positions was given in a response to the early Black Papers (*Education for Democracy*, Rubinstein and Stoneman, 1970). But the view has also been developed by radical educators such as Holt (1964), Reimer (1971), Postman and Weingartner (1971) and others who question the given nature not only of the components of the curriculum but also the institution of schooling itself; a questioning developed most notably by Illich in his famous critique *Deschooling Society* (1971)[3] wherein schooling is not only seen as an artefact but also as one that is unnecessary and even corrupting in its effects. He writes: 'school makes alienation preparatory to life, thus depriving education of reality and work of creativity and this restraint on healthy, productive and potentially independent human beings is performed by schools with an economy which only labour camps could rival'. But the constructed perspective has been even more fully articulated by sociologists drawing upon the work of the phenomenological school (Young, 1971; Wax and Wax, 1964;

Keddie, 1973) who argue that reality is a social construct; that things are as they are because we see them as such and behave accordingly. Curriculum knowledge like all other knowledge is seen not to have a permanent 'out there' nature but rather to be an artefact as are the qualities of 'truth' and 'objectivity' commonly associated with it.

The development of the reflexive ideology of the curriculum opens up fundamentally new prospects not only in sociological analysis but also in the very nature of social organization and political systems. As Whitty and Young (1976) emphasize, the development of such a perspective on the school curriculum 'could make an important contribution to the struggle for change. In particular [it] could help to get rid of the idea that what exists is the only possibility.'

It is important to emphasize that both perspectives are susceptible to sociological analysis. There is little risk of mistaking this in the reflexive perspective, many of whose advocates proclaim themselves to be wholly open to sociological investigation. Indeed, many are sociologists and justify their arguments as sociologists. The advocates of the received perspective, on the other hand, commonly seek to restrict the sociological analysis of the curriculum to the consideration of non-fundamental organizations of knowledge that have developed within the school system around and subordinate to the essential nature of knowledge. Yet the received perspective, notably its social control processes whereby individuals obtain or are denied access to knowledge and its use, offers equally important opportunities for analysis too. The use of both perspectives in the period since 1960 calls for careful scrutiny as a prelude to the study of the other related conceptual frameworks that will also require consideration in order to equip us to analyse the school curriculum sociologically.

The philosophical justification of the received perspective

At the heart of the literature of the received curriculum are the philosophical accounts of the nature of knowledge that address themselves to such fundamental issues as to what extent we may talk of subjects, disciplines, fields of studies and similar categorizations of knowledge. In the search for legitimacy in curriculum practice much effort has always been made in this area since the time of Plato. If, indeed, knowledge consists of a limited number of forms or realms that may be identified, then it offers the promise of the most impeccable case with which to counter challenges to the definition and evaluation of knowledge and even, as Plato showed, to the distribution of knowledge. Most groups holding power seek to secure their position by arguing a demonstration of knowledge; philosophers tend to become the 'official spokesmen' of such groups.

A leading contemporary exponent of this genre is Hirst, representing a group which maintains, for example, positivist distinctions between fact and value, who since 1965 has developed the concept of 'forms of knowledge' that, in his view, arise from the progressive differentiation in human consciousness of seven or eight distinguishable cognitive systems (Hirst, 1975). These forms of knowledge are classified as scientific, mathematical, religious, moral, historical, sociological and aesthetic, and consist of clusters of concepts and procedures which are specific to each form and which give rise to distinctive claims to truth in each case. Most forms of knowledge have central distinguishing features: central concepts peculiar in character to the form; a distinctive logical structure; expressions or statements which, by virtue of the form's particular terms and logic, are testable against experience; particular techniques and skills for exploring experience and testing their distinctive expressions.

There are also fields of knowledge, both theoretical and practical, that are distinguished by their subject matter rather than by a logically distinct form of expression. Within that subject matter, they draw on the disciplines as need be and are thus in a sense interdisciplinary. Geography is offered as an example of a field of theoretical study; engineering as an example of a practical study.

Though interrelated, Hirst claims that religion, literature and the fine arts in particular represent unique forms of knowledge. For Hirst the curriculum can be clearly described in terms of the forms and fields of knowledge and the formal structures that link them. This is not necessarily an advocacy by Hirst of a traditional subject-based curriculum, indeed Stenhouse suggests that Hirst is attacking rather than defending the existing subject order (Stenhouse, 1975, p. 20). Hirst does, however, require that any curriculum must remain true to the underlying forms of knowledge that of necessity it must include (though he neglects the analysis of the social consequences of such adherence that were first explored by Weber).

Hirst further argues that the fundamental purpose of education is the development of mind so that progressive distinction of forms of knowledge can be achieved by the individual for whom no experience is intelligible other than by the concepts which frame it and make it what it is. Here again he largely ignores the social context in which these processes must occur.

An essential component of Hirst's thesis is the viability of rational planning by curricular objectives. He claims 'there can be no curriculum without objects' (1975, p. 3), the objectives being determined by the forms of knowledge and the progressive development of mind by the student that is associated with them.

Faced with the 'certainty' of the nature of knowledge and the appropriate development of mind, it is but a further step to proceed from a desire to make teachers aware of the facts to an advocacy of a prescribed curriculum based upon them. Such a step has been taken not by Hirst but by White in his book *Towards a Compulsory Curriculum* (1973). White, concerned by what he sees as the unchartered consequences of individualization such as the 'bewildering variety of curricular patterns currently found in Comprehensive Schools' (p. 3), argues that children should only be constrained to study things which can be shown to be good for them as individuals or morally desirable. His case for a curriculum divided into compulsory and optional experiences is based not only on the work of Hirst but also the arguments of Peters for what he regards as 'intrinsically worthwhile activity' in the curriculum (1973).

Even without the extensions of White, Hirst's argument leads to a classic confrontation with the advocates of the constructed perspective or, as Hirst labels them, the 'social determinists'. He writes (1975, ch. 9):

> Perhaps more serious is yet another objection, that by the nature of the case at least some of the most important objectives of education, particularly in the area of the arts, cannot be specified as they are to be pupils' unique and novel achievements and responses. If what is wanted is something unique, how could it be specified or planned for? Clearly each individual result cannot be pre-specified, but equally clearly teachers must, even in the arts, have in mind a limited range of objectives of a specifiable character. The objective may be any achievement with certain features, but if there is teaching going on at all there are objectives to the enterprise. It is simply not true that teaching creative writing or poetic appreciation has no specifiable objectives. The nature of that specification of course depends entirely on what the objectives are, no one formula being suitable for all achievements. But variations of characterisation in no way undermine the claim that there always are objectives in teaching activities.

It is clear that Hirst's work is not only a theory of knowledge; it is also one of the most coherent and highly developed theories of the curriculum. It is, however, one in which the sociological analysis of the curriculum is inevitably relegated to the study of non-fundamental organizations of knowledge that have developed circumstantially within the school system. Curriculum variations for different sub-cultural groups or indeed for different ability levels form no part of Hirst's thesis. As we shall see later in the chapter, Hirst's position is fundamentally challenged by sociologists working within the reflexive perspective, notably Bourdieu (1974). But it is also challenged by writers such as Bantock (1971) who do not accept Hirst's view that there is 'no need for a radically new pattern of curricula' or that 'the central objectives of education are development of mind'. Certainly there are widespread disagreements within the received perspective between philosophers representing different power positions, for example the debate between Hirst (1965) and Phillips (1970) over the state of religious understandings.

Another well-known philosopher who, though within a given perspective, presents an alternative position, is Phenix with his *Realms of Meaning* (1964). He offers a view of knowledge that is more 'person oriented' than Hirst's, seeing human-beings as 'essentially creatures who have the power to experience *meanings*. Distinctively human existence consists in a pattern of meanings. Furthermore, *general education is the process of engendering essential meanings*' (1964, p. 5). An important feature of Phenix's view of knowledge is that its given nature in part springs from the given nature of the human mind. In Hirst's view the mind is but an instrument to allow the individual to achieve an understanding of the fundamental nature of knowledge; in Phenix's view the mind is involved itself in the creation of knowledge. However, Phenix sees mind as 'given' just as fully as knowledge itself so that then the ultimate outcome is similar to that of Hirst.[4] Certainly Phenix's concept of a real, objective world which we can discover, clarify and make meaningful is unmistakable (1962, p. 280).

There is a logos of being which it is the office of reason to discover. The structure of things is revealed, not invented, and it is the business of enquiry to open that structure to general understanding through the formation of appropriate concepts and theories. Truth is rich and varied, but it is not arbitrary. The nature of things is given, not chosen, and if man is to gain insight he must employ the right concepts and methods. Only by obedience to the truth thus discovered can he learn to teach.

In short, authentic disciplines are at one and the same time approximations to the given orders of reality and disclosures of the paths by which persons may come to realise truth in their own being, which is simply that the disciplines are the sole proper source of the curriculum.

Phenix's fundamental patterns of meanings, which it is the task of the educator to transmit, involve six possible modes or realms of human understanding.

The six realms listed as symbolics, empirics, esthetics, synnoetics, ethics and synoptics, are seen as providing 'the foundations for all the meanings that enter into human experience'. They are the foundations in the sense that they cover the pure and archetypal kinds of meaning that determine the quality of every humanly significant experience.

There are important and fundamental differences between Hirst and Phenix, notably in their classification of the 'objects of knowledge', in their conception of the process of knowing and in the distinction between 'knowledge that' and 'knowledge how', as Hirst makes clear in his chapter on the realms of meaning (1975), where he fundamentally challenges a number of Phenix's areas. Yet it is none the less clear that the work of Phenix, like that of Hirst, serves an important legitimating function to those who embrace a received curriculum.

The psychological justification of the received perspective

Another important group of curriculum theorists who may be grouped within the received ideological perspective spring from psychological origins. As we have seen, the prescriptive psychology of predictive testing and individual differences has clear implications for the distribution, evaluation and definition of the curriculum, usually serving to justify longstanding practices. Moreover, the psychologists' confidence in the certainty of their ability to identify and measure human capacities came to be matched by a similar certainty of curriculum analysts. It fell to a psychologist, Bloom (1956), to co-ordinate the establishment of the taxonomy of education objectives; a lengthy list ultimately to be divided into cognitive, affective and motor domains that was seen by him and many others as a preliminary step to the measurement of the curricular learning.

But a considerably more elegant psychological argument is that of

Bruner in his books *The Process of Instruction* (1960) and *Towards a Theory of Instruction* (1966). Bruner is not only clear that structured fields of knowledge exist; he also argues that unless the structure of and the context within such fields of knowledge are made clear, the learning process will be impaired (1966, pp. 31–2):

> Teaching specific topics of skills without making clear their context in the broader fundamental structure of a field of knowledge is un-economical in several deep senses. In the first place, such teaching makes it exceedingly difficult for the student to generalise from what he has learned to what he will encounter later. In the second place, learning that has fallen short of a grasp of general principles has little reward in terms of intellectual excitement. The best way to create interest in a subject is to render it worth knowing, which means to make the knowledge gained usable in one's thinking beyond the situation in which the learning has occurred. Third, knowledge one has acquired without sufficient structure to tie it together is knowledge that is likely to be forgotten. An unconnected set of facts has a pitiably short half-life in memory. Organising facts in terms of principles and ideas from which they may be inferred is the only known way of reducing the quick rate of loss of human memory.

There is little doubt that the fluent argument of Bruner about the underlying framework of coherence and structure of knowledge has provided, more than perhaps any other single source, the legitimation of many of the curriculum units of the past two decades, including the well-known *Man: A Course of Studies in Society*.

By including Bruner as a representative of the received perspective, we have helped to make it clear that this is not a label being used to describe a range of reactionary or even traditional orientations to the curriculum. The common basis of the case being argued by Hirst, Phenix, Bruner and many other writers whom we have grouped within the given perspective is that there are established and knowable structures of knowledge that exist independently of teachers or indeed of any other individuals; that these patterns may be discovered, clarified and comprehended, and that adherence to them is either necessary or at least highly desirable if curriculum is to be meaningful and learning experiences successful.

The socially received perspective

A variation of the received perspective sighted is the view that the curriculum is given not so much as a consequence of the nature of knowledge but of the nature of children. This may be through their psychological capacity as Bruner has suggested; an argument that has been vigorously and influentially put by Piaget with his stages of cognitive development. It may be, as Williams (1961), Thompson (1968) and many others have suggested, a consequence of their position in the social class structure or their likely future position in the occupational structure. This latter point has had a persuasive influence on educational practice since the time of Plato with his prescription of different styles of curriculum for men of gold, silver and base metal. This 'tripartite' division was endorsed in Britain in the 1940s by the Spens Committee which advocated it as the basis for the post-1944 system of secondary education to be divided into grammar, technical and modern schools.

The grammar schools were to be charged of those who, with superior intellect, were likely to proceed to the professional and higher administrative groups; through the sixth form they would be prepared for advanced further education at university and elsewhere. At the other, larger, end of the scale, the secondary modern schools would provide for the mass of workers whose intellectual attainments were seen to be modest and for whom external examinations and extended courses were unnecessary. In between there was to be a band of technical provision. The detailed arrangements were outlined in *The New Secondary Education* published by the Ministry of Education in 1947. Alongside the tripartite secondary schools, the independent fee-paying public schools were to continue to provide for the educational needs of a small elite.

The theme of a curriculum determined by occupational expectations is a recurring one. Castle (1956), in his widely read *Ancient Education and Today*, gave further currency to the view suggesting that young workers in the factories should be educated in a manner that would enable them to occupy their minds during the tedium of their everyday work.

But a considerably more sophisticated and persuasive view comes from the work of Bantock (1968), who claims that public education had up to the time of writing failed, due to attempts to impose a literary culture on the masses whose tradition is an oral, non-literary one. He advocated that there should be two kinds of curriculum, a high culture for a small minority who are academically minded and a quite different, non-literary curriculum for the masses. Subsequently Bantock (1971) gave considerable attention to the development of a suitable non-literary curriculum in which more emphasis was placed on the education of the senses. It would deal with the 'particular' rather than 'universals'; with the instinctive rather than the rational. He sees it as having a number of characteristics: concrete and specific rather than abstract; concerned with the discriminating use of the mass media, the education of the emotions and concerned with preparation for leisure. Such a liberal education should include dance and drama, art and craft and 'be aimed at the practical realities of common life'.

Bantock's suggestions have been widely criticized on the predictable grounds of his attempted differentiation between the academic minority and the non-academic masses; a distinction which even if it could be made would almost certainly be unreliable and virtually impossible to implement. There are similar objections to his belief in the possibility of clear and meaningful distinction between high and low culture. Yet there is a real problem to which Bantock has drawn attention. It is the problem of Hoggart in his *Uses of Literacy* (1960): 'It seems unlikely at any time, and is certainly not likely in any period which those of us now alive are likely to know, that a majority in any class will have strongly intellectual pursuits', yet, he continues, 'there are other ways of being in the truth'. Summarizing the debate, Lawton has written: 'the problem in terms of curriculum is thus to find a way of bridging the gap between the academic and the everyday, and not to force half digested academic ideas down unwilling throats of *all* classes and all abilities: the solution does not lie in dividing people neatly into two closed categories' (1975, p. 16).

The problems in the definition, evaluation and distribution of knowledge to which the received perspective and its variant, the socially received perspective, have alerted us are fundamental. They question the nature of social organizations and the place of schools within them, and we shall need to return to them on a number of occasions in the remaining parts of this book. But it is now necessary to present, in some detail, the justification for the reflexive perspective which throws an opposite illumination on almost all the arguments that have been considered within the received perspective.

The justification of the reflexive perspective

If the received perspective draws its strength from the support of philosophers and psychologists then those who have sought to challenge them have with almost equal regularity found support from sociologists.

Much of the dynamic of the reflexive perspective still derives from the ideas of Marx. Though in no way specifically formulated with regard to formal educational arrangements, his analysis saw societies as being characterized by ruling-class determination of the definition, evaluation and distribution of knowledge — a definition established through their control of the economic system. But a central theme of Marx was that the situation is not a given one; through an identification of the culture of the working classes and a revolutionary challenge to the ruling-class culture, a new egalitarian culture could prevail.

Yet it was Mannheim rather than Marx who focused sociological attention on the nature of knowledge and the social processes associated with its establishment and continuance. One of the clearest early articulations of the reflexive perspective was Mannheim's assertion (1936, p. 238):

> The sociology of knowledge is concerned not so much with distortions due to a deliberate effort to deceive, as with the varying ways in which objects present themselves to the subject according to the differences in social settings. Thus, mental structures are inevitably differently formed in different social and historical settings.

Mannheim's view was at once less revolutionary and more synoptic than that of Marx. In consequence he was able to assert, as did Weber, that the social backgrounds of human groups with their distinctive perspectives and distinctive perceptions ensure that groups are differentiated one from the other. In consequence limited, rather than universal, views of reality must prevail: a view of reality reinforced, according to Durkheim (1956), by different patterns of socialization taking place in different social milieux. Such relative perceptions were seen by Mannheim to account for the greater part of human knowledge, though he specifically excluded mathematics and some aspects of science from his thesis.

Like Marx, Mannheim believed that it was possible for individuals to modify their view of reality. Through conscious efforts or appropriate guidance they may come to perceive and interpret reality from a number of different positions and need not necessarily be constrained by their original ones. But for Mannheim the way to do this was through detachment from social class involvement, with all the constraints that this implied. Mannheim envisaged a model of the detached social scientist that was of course particularly attractive to the scientific aspirations of the sociologists of the 1930s. But Mannheim, like Marx, avoided the extreme relativist version of the reflexive perspective. Both implied that the new awareness or enlightenment of the individual that would arise from their advocacy was in some way superior to the position that he would have held previously.

But many social scientists have attempted to challenge even more fundamentally the received nature of knowledge. This has occurred particularly within the field of social science study itself where the received perspective has been widely embraced, often in the search for scientific respectability. Sociologists, especially, have been attracted by a range of new *interpretative* approaches to the study of knowledge variously labelled *symbolic interactionism* and *phenomenology* and *ethnomethodology*.[5]

Symbolic interactionism is concerned to explore the ways in which human beings develop knowledge, defend and benefit themselves in the way in which they present themselves to others and the constant process of adjustment made by them in this presentation. Goffman's work, for example, observes the presentation of the self in a variety of social situations such as shops, restaurants, leisure activities, as well as in closed institutions. In all he is concerned to explore the pattern of negotiations or interactions, frequently by asking such apparently simple-minded but essentially complex questions as 'how do people avoid bumping into each other on the street?'.

Such inquiries, though undeniably 'research', are fundamentally different from the controlled research design of the natural sciences, being concerned not with apparently rational, general and given knowledge and behaviour, but with non-rational, specific and often disordered understandings that seem to have little relation either to the forms of knowledge of Marx and Mannheim. Linked with symbolic interactionism is a more general phenomenology, concerned with the manner in which the individual perceives reality in social situations and responds to his perceptions. For the phenomenologists, the 'social constructions of reality' of individuals are in fact social knowledge which is seen not as having a permanent 'out there' nature but rather to be an essentially relativist artefact as are the qualities of 'truth' and 'objectivity' associated with it. It is this 'rediscovery' and reinterpretation of the sociology of knowledge that forms an important part of phenomenology which goes on to explore the processes whereby individuals obtain or are denied access to knowledge – in fact the exploration of the social control of knowledge that is largely unexamined in the given perspective. The exploration requires the examination of all that is 'taken for granted'.

Yet a further development of the reaction to positivism has been the ethnomethodological approaches concerned with 'indexicality' developed by Garfinkel (1967) and others, in which researchers are charged with a kind of experimental 'deviant participant role' in which their 'normal' patterns of response and interaction, based on this shared knowledge in a group, are deliberately broken and violated. One of the important consequences is modification, interruption or even breakdown in human interaction within the group and another may be the questioning of positivist 'received' views on the nature of knowledge.

In consideration of the reaction to the received perspective, the work of two phenomenologists, Berger and Luckmann (1971), is of particular importance in suggesting that the way in which reality is perceived in all social situations is an artefact; a construction of all the participants of a social situation which, however permanent it may appear to be, may be redefined and therefore changed. It follows that the participants take a part in defining reality in any social situation, such as the teachers and the students in the curriculum in which they are engaged. The participant's presence may significantly change the situation he is engaged in, forcing to some extent all participants to redefine it and modify their actions accordingly. Writing on this theme Gorbutt (1972, p. 8) has noted:

Clearly teachers' subject and pedagogical perspectives had implications for the way in which they organise children's learning, assess their success and so on. If we take the notion that intelligence is not an intrinsic quality of the child but is imputed to him by others then we can ask questions like how does the teacher define an intelligent child? What is the implicit concept of intelligence being used by the teacher and where did he acquire it? Are the teacher's judgments about intelligence linked to his belief about social class? Through an understanding of the socially constructed nature of teachers' subject and pedagogical perspectives and their constituent categories we can gain new insights into the determinants of teaching and learning activities in classrooms.

One of the most influential exponents of the so-called new approaches in the analysis of the curriculum has, however, been Young (1971), who brings together a number of the components of the reflexive perspective in an *interpretative paradigm* and uses this to challenge the received or normative approaches to the curriculum. For Young the sociology of education has been dominated by received approaches. Sociologists have 'taken' educators' problems as given and in their inquiries on these given problems, such as the differential achievement of curriculum knowledge by children of different social backgrounds, have accepted the educators' definition of the situation with all its assumptions of the nature and availability of knowledge and of children's abilities and social backgrounds unchallenged.

In the interpretative paradigm Young challenges such a sociology of the curriculum on the ground of its unsubstantiated and incomplete nature and also on the grounds that it allows the continuance of a process of social control that he regards as unacceptable and distorting. Yet the extent to which the interpretative paradigm develops the reflexive view of knowledge is, as Lawton (1975, p. 58) notes, somewhat unclear. Lawton suggests that there are five different levels of development:

Level 1: That the present structure and organisation of education in our society serves to preserve the *status quo* in an unjust society — this level is particularly concerned with questions such as the *social distribution of knowledge.*

Level 2: That in particular the *content* of education — the selection of knowledge for transmission by schools — should be *made* into a problem for critical examination rather than be taken for granted; this level is concerned with *what counts for knowledge in our society, and the stratification of knowledge.*

Level 3: That *subject barriers are arbitrary and artificial*, existing largely for the convenience of those in control of education.

Level 4: That *all knowledge is socially constructed.*

Level 5: That not only knowledge but *rationality itself is merely a convention.*

Certainly statements that appear to indicate a commitment to all levels are to be found in Young's collection of papers (though not in the papers of all his contributors). Together they raise a powerful series of questions on the whole nature and practice of the received or normative curriculum and in this alone provide a compelling justification for the formulation of the interpretative paradigm. Why, for example, they ask, do we still continue to provide a curriculum at which working-class children regularly and predictably fail? Why can most of the curriculum be divided unhesitatingly into higher-status subjects such as mathematics, literature and pure science and lower-status subjects such as home economics, woodwork and gardening and why do most working-class children tend to find themselves taking combinations of predominantly lower-status subjects whereas middle-class children tend to take combinations of predominantly higher-status subjects?

Young's arguments and those of his fellow contributor Esland (1971) leave little doubt about the persisting strength of the received perspective in the school curriculum and the persistence of elitist orientations in the determination, evaluation and distribution of knowledge. Moreover, their questions and particularly the analysis of classroom behaviour by Keddie (1971) offer some illuminating indications of the way that the received perspective is perpetuated not only through the existence of an effective, even if ill-defined, elite but also through the day-to-day activities of teachers and even of pupils. This occurs in the way in which they perceive and structure knowledge and define its suitability or unsuitability for different categories of children. We shall discuss this in greater detail in the next chapter.

The received and reflexive perspectives juxtaposed

Although the arguments of the interpretative paradigm about the nature of the curriculum have a compelling face validity, its comments on the relative nature of knowledge are at best inconclusive and unsubstantiated particularly at the higher level of Lawton's categorization. The extreme relativist position advocated, however inconsistently, in Young's book, suffers from precisely the same problems as the extreme determinist position discussed within the context of the given perspectives. Indeed, Brent, in a paper on 'The Sociology of Knowledge and Epistemology' (1975), has drawn attention to some of the links between the two perspectives with particular reference to the work of Hirst and Berger and Luckmann. Certainly if the work of Hirst and Phenix is sociologically vulnerable then the work of Young and Esland is equally vulnerable philosophically. At the extreme both fail to do justice to each other's position in that they ignore each other and in so doing ignore important aspects of social reality. One of the persistent omissions of the received perspective is its not infrequent failure to account for deviations from the 'true' patterns or distribution of knowledge. One of the persistent omissions of the relativist perspective is its failure to account for the regularities that so visibly occur in individuals' construction of reality. No matter how relatively based, strong recurring and identifiable patterns of knowledge exist in all human groups and in all societies. Not only social organizations but most human behaviour in recognizable forms would cease were it not so. Furthermore, as we have seen, every society has restrictions on the access to at least part of its knowledge that is variously defined as sacred, professional, privileged or restricted to those who have satisfied certain training or membership criteria. Though not 'given' or received in the fullest sense in which we have used the term in this chapter, none the less the *de facto* experience of individuals in relation to such knowledge is as if it were given.

This is not to say that definitions, evaluations and distribution of knowledge cannot change and are given for all time. Kuhn (1970) has reminded us that even in science, an area held apart by Mannheim, patterns of knowledge can and do change radically. New authorities, such as Keynes in the field of economic analysis, may emerge to answer problems that cannot be solved within the existing pattern and if they are successful the field may be *restructured* around them. But it is always a restructuring in which much of the previous pattern can be seen to remain. Kuhn also reminds us of the immense power of the patterns of knowledge during their established period in each area. Though he writes specifically of science there is little difficulty in extrapolating his comments through the range of subject areas. All of them contain a present stock of relevant substantive and theoretical knowledge; the definitions of what is accepted truth and what is questionable. With the aid of the control strategies that we have noted in previous chapters, they define, often precisely, where research may be undertaken, the kinds of new books that may be written, the kinds of teaching that will be acceptable. The penalty for deviance for the student or faculty member may be examination failure, non-publication of his papers, unemployment and even public ridicule.

The situation in schools is in many ways parallel to the university situation portrayed by Kuhn. The advocate of the 'heretical' thesis in the university is unlikely to obtain his doctorate; then so the person advocating a deviant curriculum in the school is likely to find his tenure distinctly less secure than heretofore − his activities 'sent up' in the local newspaper. The history of all education systems contains evidence of the personal sacrifice that accompanies deviancy. Yet for many teachers in universities, colleges and schools, the constraints are not ones of which they are sharply aware. Their internalization of the received perspective that surrounds their work is sufficient to ensure that they are only infrequently conscious of their constraints. And most teachers do not need reminding that their own authority and role also spring from the existing social order; that to challenge the system is to challenge their own present position.

It follows that for the average schoolteacher planning and executing his school curriculum, reality is likely to be far removed from the extreme positions we have outlined for the received and the reflexive perspectives. Both perspectives in their extreme forms are unlikely to be able to offer him a convincing demonstration that reality for him is likely to be other than he knows it. Neither are likely to pay detailed attention to the day-to-day realities of his position in the curriculum. But at a lower level of assertion both perspectives offer a more useful service for the practitioner. They encourage him to ask why it is that things are the way they are; what is the social significance of his timetable or his marking system, or even why he persists in transmitting knowledge in a form that is manifestly unlike either the forms or realms of knowledge described by Hirst or Phenix.

Towards a restructuring perspective

At this point the two perspectives have jointly led us back to the issue with which we began this chapter, the school curriculum and the exercise of power. It is now clear that this is built upon two elements: the consciousness of those who participate in the curriculum, notably the teachers, and the objective realities of the social and curriculum structure in which they exist. The distinction between consciousness and structure is an important one, as Marx and Engels emphasize in *The German Ideology* (1964).

But to emphasize one or other alone is to risk distortion. The emphasis on consciousness that is central to the reflexive perspective can conceal the important underlying structure of relationships; the emphasis on structure inherent in the received perspective can hide the capacity of individuals to impose their definitions on the situation. Marx, recognizing both elements, employed an analysis in which both were brought together through examining the basic structural forms and the way in which individuals, finding themselves within these structures, experience both opportunities and constraints. Sharp and Green (1975, pp. 27–8), commenting on these issues, write:

Although determinism may be inappropriate as a generalized perspective this does not mean that social reality never affects the individual as if it were a mechanistic determining force, especially those at low levels of the social structure, far from the mechanisms of power and control. We argue therefore that the correct perspective should enable one to ask the question 'Under what historical conditions can men break through the structure of determinations?'

At this point we can present the concept of a *restructuring perspective* — a perspective in which both received and reflexive perspectives can be brought together as two related modes of understanding both the realities of knowledge in the school curriculum and the possibilities of change therein. It is a perspective in which we may pay particular attention to the realities of the exercise of power in the curriculum and the consequences of that exercise in the wider society. Essentially the issue to which the restructuring perspective can address itself is a simple one. How may the curriculum not only assist a wider range of students to enhance their expectations of power and their capacity to exercise it but also play its part in bringing about a social situation in which these expectations and capacities may be used?

As a means of demonstrating the usefulness of a restructuring perspective let us consider first of all what Gorbutt (1972) rightly regards as a primary focus within the received perspective of the sociology of education — 'the differential performance of working-class children as compared with middle-class children in educational institutions'; in short, the discontinuity of knowledge between the working-class home and the school. Gorbutt points out that from the standpoint of the reflexive perspectives we can see that 'underlying this explanation is a notion of cultural deficit which implies that working-class culture is not only different but deficient and inferior. Thus a value judgment about the worthwhileness of a particular culture is being made by a supposedly value free social science.'

Gorbutt, like Brandis and Henderson (1970, pp. 122–3) before him, offers a good example of a reflexive construction that is powerfully reinforced by a received one that reminds us that the ways in which curriculum knowledge is defined and evaluated by the teacher are of critical importance to the achievement and life chance of children. In turn the reflexive perspective can continue to remind us that achievement

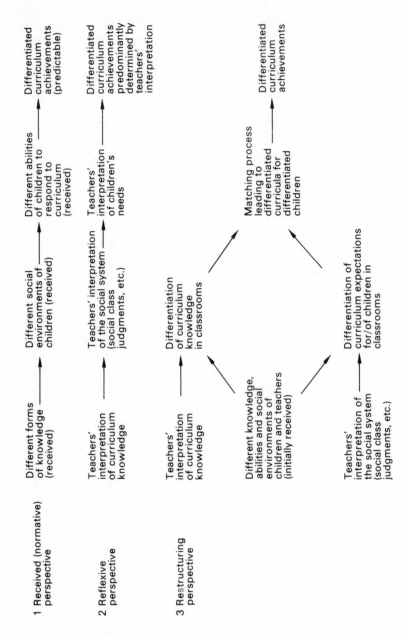

Figure 2   *Explanations for curriculum achievement*

and life chance are themselves socially determined categories. While this interplay has been implicit in a number of well-known studies, at least from the time of Douglas's work (1964) onwards, the new emphasis leads to considerable enhancement of the understanding of the experience of schooling and a broadening of the analysis that goes well beyond the middle-class/working-class dissonance. Becker (1963), in particular, has demonstrated that, at least in theory, any category of student can be defined as estranged or disadvantaged from whatever the prevailing view of knowledge of the teacher happens to be.

But it is important to emphasize that this restructuring of our understanding of curriculum knowledge has occurred incrementally. Using the problem area of achievement in the curriculum to which we have been alerted by Gorbutt, let us, at the risk of some oversimplification, set out in a diagram (Figure 2) the ways in which the three perspectives of curriculum knowledge may contribute to our understanding. Figure 2 demonstrates the incremental relationship between the perspectives in that 2 has developed from 1 and 3 from 2. It also demonstrates the relationship between the contributions of the three perspectives. In particular, it shows one of the central tenets of the received perspective; the dominance of teachers' perceptions and the way in which in the restricting perspective these perceptions are augmented by new evidence from the children and the teachers.

The potential of the restructuring perspective in the analysis of curriculum is considerable. It has obvious use in examining both the received and reflexive assumptions underlying compensatory education and curricula for non-academic school leavers. It offers the opportunity for a clearer look at components such as teacher behaviour and important concepts such as power – until now underplayed in both perspectives. Though we have reached the restructuring perspective incrementally it can and will be used independently: its critical capacity exists and can be used without further rehearsal of the shortcomings of the perspectives from which it was developed. The wisdom of the restructuring perspective springs fundamentally not from the received or reflexive thesis but from history. Armed with the restructuring perspective we can proceed to consider, in the subsequent chapters, the organization and practice of the curriculum in the school system.

Summary

Springing from the historical analysis of the curriculum in the previous chapter we identified two contrasting ideological perspectives – the *received perspective* (with its variant the *socially received perspective*) and the *reflexive perspective* of knowledge.

The development of these perspectives in recent years was reviewed, particular attention being given to the *interpretative paradigm* advocated by sociologists working within the reflexive perspective. After juxtaposing the perspectives, elements of both were incorporated into a *restructuring perspective* to be used to analyse the practice of curriculum in the school.

Curriculum organization in the school - the teachers' role

If we look at the working world of the school the scene appears to be far removed from the complex theoretical world that we have just been considering. Within the school the complexities appear to be of a very different kind. At one moment we are likely to find the inhabitants, strangely clad, co-operating in teams to defeat their adversaries, fighting nearly to the death on the games field. At other times one can see them engaged in keen individual competition against each other in the examination room. Certainly an observer from some remote society would be intrigued by the behaviour of the adults in the schools, performing roles quite unlike those existing elsewhere. They may be leading symbolic acts of corporate worship, encouraging the learning of algebraic manipulations and the history of neolithic man, building spaceships with eggboxes, blowing whistles, ringing bells, clapping hands and above all claiming, usually successfully, authority over the young. Asked to identify themselves, the adults would label themselves as teachers — as teachers of children, of an age group, of an ability group or most characteristically as subject teachers — still the strongest bastion of identity throughout the school system. Geer (1966) has demonstrated the importance of curriculum identity within the occupational commitment of the teaching profession and Musgrove (1968) has emphasized the sense of identity conferred by subjects.

Perhaps the least likely activity for a teacher would be to sit in the corner of the staffroom, pondering anxiously whether or not the ideological foundations of his work were based upon received or reflexive ideological perspectives. Indeed it is highly likely that many of the teachers would have never even heard of the forms of knowledge or even of the interpretative paradigm. Unless by chance they were following an in-service programme or an Open University course the names of Phenix, Bantock, Hirst or Young might mean little to them. Faced with

75

the pressing day-to-day curricular problems of discipline, marking children's work, preparing laboratory practicals, maintaining supplies of books and stationery and keeping *au fait* with the requirements of the examination boards, do teachers really have the opportunity, let alone the incentive, to concern themselves with ideology in their day-to-day curricular organizations?

Does the teacher make curriculum decisions?

To begin to answer the question, let us turn to the primary school classrooms. Here one is likely to find many examples of curricula in which fairly frequent organizational decisions are required by the teachers, who have to interpret what is appropriate for the various children in the classroom at the various stages in the school day. Sometimes the pattern of events may be so spontaneous and so flexible that almost all behaviour seems to spring from the teacher's interpretation of the social situation in the classroom; that the received or even the reflexive perspective has no place in the explanation of events. A representative example of such a curriculum is to be seen in the account of Miss Sanders and her response to Donnie, a boy with a broken arm. It is drawn from an advertisement for educational films in an American educational technology magazine which commences with a picture of Donnie and continues:

> You're all hanging up your coats at school and in comes Donnie with a cast on his arm. Everybody has to see it and touch it and write on it. 'How long do you have to wear it, Donnie?' 'Miss Sanders, what makes bones?' 'How can you break your arm swimming?' 'Will it grow back, Miss Sanders?' This is the teachable moment. It's the rare moment when you really want to learn. But your curiosity sure isn't satisfied by seeing just the cast. You want to see inside. So somebody goes to the film library and brings back a film selection on bones. You put it in the projector and — wow — a great movie. This way Miss Sanders can teach you all kinds of things — more things than anyone would expect her to know — at the exact moment when you want to learn them. And it's alive, the way you're used to seeing it.

Miss Sanders in this example, appears to be totally responsive to the immediate situation of the children. Whilst it would be perhaps unfair to label her as opportunist she is highly likely to respond with different but equal enthusiasm the next morning when the pipe-layers commence work on the new water main in the road outside the school or the birds nest in the school roof. There seems little doubt that, in her classroom, she is sovereign and that her construction of reality is the major determinant of what takes place.

The model of Miss Sanders is not confined to the primary school classroom. The search for individual spontaneity in the arts studio or in the creative writing workshop of the secondary school is in a very similar way apparently a product of the shared consciousness of teachers and children with a curriculum that appears to be a response to the perceptions of the participants at the time and which seems to bear little relationship to that which takes place under the heading of art or writing in other schools or even within the same school at different times. Similarly the non-directive teaching strategies characteristic of the Humanities Curriculum Project or the Oxford Moral Education Project seem to involve curricula that are spontaneous and collectively determined rather than received in any sense. The discussion sessions in the liberal studies programmes in the colleges of further education are likely to fall into a similar category, as are many components of the newly established individual studies programmes at universities in Britain and North America.

Certainly such curricula lack the predictability of more traditional curriculum organizations and the ensuing difficulties of supervision add a further dimension of freedom to the teacher's organization of curriculum. The issue of supervision is indeed a major one. The possibility and, arguably, the need for supervision are important corollaries of the concept of the received curriculum. In the recent past a headteacher or a head of department could expect to know, in fairly considerable detail, the curriculum of most of the subjects in his school or department and the appropriate stage to be reached by the various categories of students. With such knowledge he could usually exercise a substantial degree of control, formally and informally, to ensure that a teacher was 'on the right lines' appropriate to his subject and age and ability group. But control of this kind becomes increasingly difficult to exercise for a number of reasons. The often considerable changes in curriculum content due to curriculum development and research by local and national agencies, sometimes by the schools themselves, has made many subjects sufficiently different, by allowing many varied 'paths', that it is only the individual teacher who can claim with 'authority' what are 'the right lines' for his class.

Alongside this there is the move from homogeneous ability groups in first, middle and secondary schools and the subsequent move towards classes that are wide-ranging in ability and, occasionally, in age too. There is also the widespread emphasis on teacher evaluation wherein teachers are encouraged not only to determine their objectives and methodology but also to undertake the assessment of what takes place in their classroom, without necessary reference to external assessment, as a personal professional responsibility. It is not only in the day-to-day organization of the curriculum in the classroom that the authority structure of the school becomes more complex and less predictable. Hoyle (1971) has drawn attention to the complexity of the problem. He contrasted the high degree of control over policy enjoyed by the headteacher and his low degree of control over how the teacher actually functions in the classroom compared with the high degree of autonomy enjoyed by the teacher in his own classroom and his relatively low degree of involvement in policy making or goal setting in the school. Richardson (1973), in her research on the organization of a large comprehensive school, draws attention to the way in which the head, senior staff and junior staff found it desirable, even necessary, to undertake the difficult tasks of co-operating in the shared solution of even the major administrative issues of the school in a way that appears to embody many elements of the reflexive perspective.

There are many other factors that appear to confirm an almost inexorable move to a reflexive curriculum, offering reassurance to the advocates of the interpretative paradigm that events are moving their way. The changing role of both Her Majesty's Inspectors and local authority inspectors to become advisers in the fullest sense of the word, offering advice and assistance rather than guidance and control (Edmonds, 1962), is certainly relevant; so too are the changing emphases of teacher training and in-service courses wherein the earlier emphases on conformity to a prescribed professional role give way to those in which initiative, originality and individuality are favoured. Promotion within the profession at all levels tends to come more easily to a teacher who 'makes a name' with his innovative and original interpretation of curriculum. The radical arguments of Reimer (1971), Postman and Weingartner (1971) and others in favour of community-centred and, frequently, anti-establishment curricula are taken heed of by many teachers, especially those faced with the unmistakable difficulties and handicaps of the deprived children in their classes in the inner city areas.

We have sketched a picture in which the reflexive curriculum based upon interpretations of teachers seems to be in the ascendency. The changing organization and management of schools, the changing social structure, the pressures of curriculum change and of professional autonomy; all these add up to what appears to be an unassailable case for a dominant reflexivity. To be sure there are many schools in which long-standing subject orientations and methodologies still prevail but even here there is often less certainty and a prospect of rapid change in the face of comprehensive school reorganization. Even though ideological consideration may seldom occur manifestly, the latent ideology of the reflexive curriculum seems to be strongly in evidence. Even though they do not consciously espouse it, many teachers actively seek to further it in their day-to-day curriculum organization. Certainly there are many who see the demise of the received curriculum as a *fait accompli* with all its implications for professional autonomy, the definition of knowledge and the practice of social control in society.

Does 'society' make curriculum decisions?

Is this the total picture or is it a gross oversimplification of reality? Let us now consider some evidence that may support the 'received' perspective. We have already taken note of Bernstein's reminder that 'How a society selects, classifies, distributes, transmits and evaluates the educational knowledge it considers to be public reflects both the distribution of power and the principles of social control' (Bernstein, 1975). Certainly Bernstein considers that the curriculum still acts as a powerful instrument of social control and a number of writers within the interpretative paradigm acknowledge that teachers often still have strongly held given views about 'the way things should be' that they impose upon their pupils through the curriculum.

For a perceptive illustration of the day-to-day practice of the given curriculum and the social control procedures inherent within it we may look at the picture painted by Hanson (1973) of the Royal Wedding Project. In his satirical paper, Hanson drew attention to the way in which, at the time, many schools were running curriculum projects on the marriage of Princess Anne and Captain Mark Phillips. With tongue in cheek he made a number of suggestions whereby teachers could enhance their projects. But his discussion also drew attention to several fundamental phenomena. The present writer's own experiences confirm that, without any official directive, very large numbers of autonomous teachers up and down the country had spontaneously decided to undertake a project on this event and, what is more, appeared to be doing so with remarkable similarity. Another and perhaps even more important feature was the way in which the projects transmitted unambiguously messages on the social structure of contemporary Britain. There was recurring emphasis on the nature of the traditional wedding service and its implications and on the role of the established church (at least two of the lessons on these themes seen by the present writer were in fact being conducted by teachers who had asked, on moral grounds, to be excused from timetabled teaching of religious education). Most discussions of the event emphasized the longstanding position of the royal family in the social system and the other divisions in the social status system. Children were shown that, at the ceremony, high-status people were occupying the front rows, lesser categories were farther away from the central aisle. More significantly children quickly came to realize that for the vast majority of people the best hope was for a place to stand outside. Pupils were not only coming to recognize the hierarchical division of society but also to recognize that their place was in most cases on the street along the procession route.

Over the years there is little doubt that teachers have been highly effective in such situations. Acceptance of the social system — its institutions, divisions, behaviour and constraints and privileges — is almost total. Certainly the future of Princess Anne and Mark Phillips is as assured as almost any institution as evidenced by the widespread feelings of dismay that greeted the attack on the royal couple in London some six months after the wedding. But the Royal Wedding Project is but one example of a continuing process. As Hanson perceptively reminded us, the next stage, in almost all schools, would be the commencement of the Christmas Project.

It is possible to suggest further examples of the process of social control and particularly of social differentiation in the secondary school. We have already referred to mathematics teaching (p. 15). Here is a subject that, ostensibly, is so important that every child must experience it, usually at least once each day. Yet at the end of secondary schooling, considerable numbers of children have achieved a level of mathematical competence that would be more appropriate to the end of their primary schooling. If the success rate is so low why is it that schools persist in the exercise? One explanation could be that if social differentiation is to take place children must be able to see it as 'legitimate'. The experience of mathematics could be very appropriate for this purpose. Pupils have the chance to see that there is a high-status group of those who can 'do' mathematics and another, often larger, group of lower-status people who, though they appear to have had the chance to join the high-status group, have failed to make it. Differentiation in such circumstances appears to be not only fair but also objective. Much the same could be said about most of the 'high-status subjects' of the curriculum; modern languages in particular constituting a similar case to mathematics. The differentiation is of course a social selection process controlling opportunities for adult status and life chance. Commonly it is also a socially reinforcing one in which children from 'superior' social backgrounds legitimate their superior prospects. The process within the school where this linked 'management of knowledge' and social control takes place is subtle but astonishingly effective and seems to occur with as much regularity in the comprehensive school as it did in the selective secondary schools of earlier decades. In all this it is important to notice that the socialization and differentiation is not only about the facts and skills contained in the curriculum but also the values within it — values that are seen to be appropriate to the future life experiences of the children in the social system — future life experiences that are in part being made different by the very experience of the curriculum.

Which of the two models of curriculum is nearer the truth? In presenting examples of practice in both 'received' and 'reflexive' frameworks, an attempt has been made to juxtapose the compulsive nature of both analyses. Let us now try to relate them, using the restructuring perspective of the previous chapter. Take the case of Miss Sanders: it is a fairly safe prediction that her treatment of the incident with Donnie will be to embark upon a fairly conventional and supportive account of our present systems for dealing with accidents. She will describe the hospital that treated Donnie and emphasize strongly the high-status professional role of the doctors who will have handled the fracture. She will probably also have mentioned the nurses indicating, perhaps in subtle ways, that their status, though high, is somewhat less than that of the doctors. She will have uttered socially reinforcing messages about the need for accident prevention and the areas of the social system where particular caution is needed.

Constraints on teachers' curriculum decisions

But if Miss Sanders does by any chance espouse markedly radical approaches in her development of inquiry learning she is likely to find herself subject to a range of controls. Some of these may be 'external', and even spectacular, as several celebrated recent cases have demonstrated where professional, community and administrative pressures have effectively brought teachers into line or else excluded them from the school. A recent case was reported on the front page of a teachers' magazine (*The Teacher*, 1975):

TEACHER CRITIC SUSPENDED

A young teacher who has attacked his school and colleagues in the press for two years, was suspended from duty by his governors on Tuesday, and asked to appear before them at the meeting next month. The governors' action defused a serious situation in which the teacher had alienated virtually every other teacher at the school. The staff had earlier decided they could no longer teach with him.

An example known to the writer was in a community service project in a 'twilight' area which constitutes the school's catchment area. The senior pupils had a local reputation for indifferent or even anti-social behaviour. A young teacher with these senior pupils undertook an impressive programme of socially approved activity whereby the boys and girls created and ran a playground, dug old people's gardens, painted their walls, cleared the local brook of debris and generally brought acceptable improvements to a rundown area. There was widespread social approval for the project; the pupils were widely praised. The civic leaders visited them; the local newspaper featured them. The teacher soon received a graded post. But events did not end there; the teacher and his pupils began to realize that the old people still had fundamental problems that could not be solved by direct action alone. They had difficulty in obtaining their rent rebate, the local council was tardy in the repair of roofs and blocked drains and other maintenance of a kind that was beyond the scope of children. With the teacher the children decided that some further action was needed and wrote to the local housing committee and to the local newspaper about the problems urging immediate action. The response was different in nature from that which they had enjoyed previously. This time the local paper was distinctly unenthusiastic about their 'interference' and redefined them as a group of teenage trouble-makers led by a 'radical' teacher. The coincidence that the chairman of the local housing committee was also a member of the local education committee appeared to lead to several problems with the school. Certainly the teacher was encouraged not to continue with this particular line of action and the project was discontinued.

Here we have reached one of the fundamental truths of the reflexive perspective; that the curriculum is about the distribution of power. The community service project offered previously powerless adolescents the chance to exercise power in society. In its first phase this presented no 'problem'; they were being given no more than the power to conform more effectively within the existing social system and to refrain from destructive activities. In the second phase they came to exercise a power to challenge some aspects of the existing system; in so doing they were, inevitably, challenging some of those who already held power therein. Not surprisingly this challenge was resisted; the existing holders of power in the community demonstrated the extent to which they were able to control curriculum. Yet while the reflexive perspective serves an important purpose in achieving such an interpretation, it offers little assistance in suggesting the way in which curriculum may be developed in the light of these realities. With the aid of the restructuring perspective we shall return to these issues in subsequent chapters.

The more usual constraints on 'Miss Sanders' are, however, even less visible. Her own upbringing, reinforced by appropriate professional socialization in the teachers' college or university department, will have gone a long way to ensure that she is not only willing but even enthusiastic to encourage her pupils to learn and internalize established social norms. The pervasive nature of professional socialization in institutions of initial training is well illustrated by Taylor in his account of English teachers' colleges (1969). The strength of such constraints on Miss Sanders's curriculum organization is likely to be unmistakable; even in the educational priority area first school where she may be working with very young children, it is likely that the play equipment she favours will be of the kind supplied by firms such as Galt and Abbatt — a kind that is also found in most middle-class homes. Certainly there is likely to be little resemblance to the 'undemanding' toys previously experienced by the majority of the children in her class (Bernstein and Young, 1967). Her expectations of their capacity to use the equipment are likely to be equally dissonant. Children's imaginative, original and unguided use of the equipment to create a variety of 'situations' would be likely to win her warm support: behaviour more likely to be rapidly achieved by middle-class children who are not only familiar with the equipment but also the 'inner directed' ethic which teaches them that adults are supportive rather than directive. This is likely to be in contrast to the expectations of many children at the other end of the social scale who, initially at least, may be 'other directed', expecting adults to tell them what to do. Similarly, the result of Miss Sanders's painting sessions with large sheets of papers, bold colours and non-representational drawing are likely to achieve a ready understanding in the minds of middle-class parents fresh from reading of the mysteries of children's art in a recent issue of *Where*; they may be greeted with frustrated incomprehension by other parents. To paraphrase Baratz and Baratz (1970), the concept of discovery methods for the underprivileged is conceptualized against the norms for middle-class children. The very subtlety of her communications with parents that carefully avoid old-fashioned crude evaluative terms about children's performances may be missed, misunderstood and wasted by many of the non-middle class to whom they are particularly addressed.

Social control in the classroom

We have painted a picture in which some of the social control aspects of the curriculum are to be seen. Occasionally these may be imposed on the teacher. More usually the social control arises from within the teacher. Let us now consider in more detail the day-to-day exchanges of the classroom and study 'Miss Sanders' in action. She may begin with a clear awareness that her own authority and role are founded securely on the existing system; that to challenge the system is to challenge her own personal position. This too has its own consequences, as Keddie (1971) has made abundantly clear.

> For the teacher, social control may depend on his being able in the classroom to maintain publicly his definition of the situation. He may do this by attempting to render pupil definitions invalid. Thus he may treat pupils' complaints about the course with scepticism and subsume them under normal categories like: 'he's trying to get out of work', 'it's just a bit of "agro" ', 'they'll try anything on'. These explanations may or may not coincide with pupils' explanations of their motives. The general effect of teachers' explanations is to recognise the situation as conflictual, but to render invalid the particular point the pupil is making and thus to delineate the extent of pupils' rights. Equal rights are not granted to all pupils since the 'same' behaviour may have different meanings attributed to it, depending on the normal status of the pupil. In one C stream lesson a pupil asked the teacher:
> Pupil: This is geography, isn't it? Why don't we learn about where countries are and that?

Teacher: This is socialisation.

Pupil: What's that? I'd rather do geography . . . Netsilik Eskimo —
I don't know where that is.

Teacher (ironically): After the lesson we'll go and get the atlas and
I'll show you.

A few days earlier I had asked this teacher whether any pupil had
asked in class (as they had in some other classes): 'Why should we do
social science?' and had had the reply:

Teacher: No, but if I were asked by Cs I would try to sidestep it because it would be the same question as 'Why do anything? Why
work?'

Observer: What if you were asked by an A group?

Teacher: Then I'd probably try to answer.

Here we see once again examples of teacher behaviour which differen-
tiates curriculum between different categories of pupil, a differentiation
reified by the repeated interactions of teacher and pupils:

Once pupils are placed in high-ability groups the wish to achieve at
school in the school's terms is confirmed and situated in school activities, and is reinforced by their long-term vocational expectations.
These are the pupils in the study who when asked about the humanities course in general terms show they tend to see it in the terms in
which teachers define it. These pupils are more likely to move
towards using the language of the subject as the teacher presents it,
and, equally important, their behavioural style is more likely to seem
to the teacher appropriate to the occasion, than the style of C
pupils. Once pupils are accredited by streaming or some other device
as of high ability, their questions are likely to be scanned by teachers
for a different kind of meaning and to be used to a different end
from those of C pupils.[1]

In the same paper Keddie offers examples of how teachers reinforce
role expectations in society through their curriculum in a lesson based
on materials designed to show that traditional roles are cultured not
biological and therefore given to discussion:

Teacher: No, (women) feel the same pain but they have a greater
resistance to it.

Boy: What are they always crying for?

Teacher: Well that's temperament, isn't it? Anyway we're getting
away from the point about the Eskimos aren't we?

Here the teacher's definition of relevance eliminates a question which would appear to offer a perfect example of the point of the curriculum material in use. Delamont (1976) offers a further example of teacher control of the curriculum situation:

> Consider the following incident from a lesson on the history of the Napoleonic wars which followed material on British politicians of the period. As soon as the whole group had assembled:
> Evelyn puts up her hand. Mrs. Flodden acknowledges it, and asks what she wants.
> Evelyn: I've got an epigram about Burke. Can I read it?
> Mrs. F. says yes 'of course'. Evelyn reads her epigram and gets laughter from the class.
> Mrs. F gets Evelyn to write it on the board so anyone who chooses can copy it down. Then announces 'notes on the Napoleonic wars'.
>
> This is an ordinary classroom exchange which, at first glance, has no features worthy of comment. However, it shows, as almost every other exchange shows, who really controls lesson content. As the lesson opens Evelyn makes a contribution relevant to the previous lesson. She offers an epigram. Note that by *offering* it, she implies she has no natural right to teach the class, she asks permission. (We can assume that, because Evelyn feels confident enough to offer her epigram, Mrs. Flodden is likely to accept it — not all teachers receive such offers.) Mrs. Flodden grants her the privilege — and then immediately 'colonises' it. She tells Evelyn to put the verse on the board, and so defines it as a piece of information that can be officially recorded. It is not, however, so important that writing it down is compulsory as the notes on the Napoleonic Wars are. By implication, therefore, Mrs. Flodden defines the epigram as marginal to history, the notes central.

But when Miss Sanders becomes aware of the discontinuities that spring from her practice and endeavours to compensate further she may yet find problems. One solution is to adopt curricula that appear to be more closely related to the lives and conditions of the local community. Indeed there have been many suggestions that the greater part of her whole curriculum could be closely linked to the everyday life situations occurring within the school catchment area. *Society and the Young School Leaver* (Schools Council, 1968) suggests a list of topics that could facilitate a move to an 'inquiry' curriculum of this kind rather than a conventional subject curriculum. The list included the family, homes, work experience in factories, myself and the world, authority-figures, the 97 bus, the water supply, the problem of colour, epidemics, clothes and other topics.

The 97 bus

But what are the implications of such a curriculum? White (1968), in a well-known article, has explored some of the possible consequences. He writes:

> One of the proposed areas of inquiry, 'The 97 Bus', will serve as an example here. This is a scheme in which children explore the workings of this bus route in depth, sometimes going off on individual assignments, recording the numbers, getting on and off the bus, interviewing people waiting for the bus to find out why they use it, visiting the bus garage to see a 97 being cleaned, to talk to the cleaners, the manageress of the canteen, inspectors and so on, and sometimes listening to outside visitors – bus drivers and conductors, regular users of the bus, the police officer responsible for traffic – who come to the school to talk about their problems.
>
> Now there is a clear appeal here to children's interests: there is the fascination of buses themselves, the chance to spend the afternoon in the fresh air interviewing people rather than in the classroom. As motivational devices these look like starters. But what are the pupils being motivated to do? What is the project aiming at? One main aim, we are told, is to help them 'to become familiar with the district in which they live, and to appreciate some of the benefits and problems of their own locality'. But how is this alleged need – to become familiar with one locality in this way – to be justified educationally?
>
> One's first reaction is to wonder why this familiarity should be singled out at all. For much of what the pupils study in this project they are already familiar with: they already know a good deal about why people travel on buses or what the job of the conductor involves. But perhaps this is to miss the point: perhaps what children come to know is not the main thing. As the working paper points out: 'the end product for the young school leaver is to be measured in terms of values and attitudes and the ability to learn rather than an exact body of knowledge'.
>
> In other words, one could well construe 'The 97 Bus' project as

an attempt to get the pupils not so much to become familiar with their locality, as to accept it as an interesting and desirable place in which to live. One could construe the outings on the buses as ways of getting pupils to appreciate facets of their physical and human environment which they would otherwise have overlooked, to see the dull streets in which they live under a new aspect, as of absorbing interest. The peeps behind the scenes at the bus garage may be interpreted as ways of encouraging the pupils to look favourably on bus driving or maintenance as a possible career.

There is evidence elsewhere in the paper that such acceptance is the primary aim. In a work experience project, for instance, pupils are not taken round factories as an organised tour, but are allocated to departments, where their careers tutor comes to talk to them as an interested visitor. 'In this way both independence and temporary identification with the firm's interests are fostered in each pupil.' Other projects place a similar stress on accepting authority by seeing what things look like from authority's point of view.

The teachers' accounting system

But there may be fundamental problems that still lie in the path of the teacher who has read Delamont, Keddie and White and is sensitive to their cautionary studies. An important example may arise in her *accounting system*, the vocabulary of reflexive education which she uses to account, to herself and to others, the meanings of her curriculum practice. Sharp and Green (1975) suggest that the available vocabulary is an inadequate tool not necessarily providing 'clear explanations or legitimations which can bridge the gap between their substantive practice on the one hand and their educational aims on the other'.

But more fundamentally they suggest that the vocabulary is of crucial importance in 'the maintenance of social control and commitment to the underlying political structure of staff relationships'. The two points are clearly illustrated in an interview with 'Mrs Carpenter', a class teacher with reflexive orientations who had recently switched from a formal mathematics curriculum:

> When you've got a set plan . . . everything in its place . . . you
> taught length immediately after you taught so and so, and it was
> taught, you know, it was not a matter of children learning really,
> not in the way we'd been thinking that they should be learning. . . .

Interviewer: How do you mean?

Teacher: I mean we all, well, I have a little plan but I don't really
. . . I just sort of, mmm, try and work out what stages each child
is at and take it from there.

Interviewer: How do you do this? How does one notice what stage a
child is at?

Teacher: Oh we don't really know, you can only say the stage he
isn't at really, because you know when a child doesn't know but
you don't really know when he knows. Do you see what I mean?
You can usually tell when they don't know (long pause). (There
was a distraction in the interview at this point.) What was I talking about?

Interviewer: Certain stages, knowing when they know —

Teacher: — and when they don't know. But even so, you still don't
know when they really don't (pause) you can't really say they
don't know, can you? . . . That's why really that plan they wanted wouldn't have worked. I wouldn't have been able to stick to
it, because you just don't . . . you know when they don't know,
you don't know when they know.

Sharp and Green present an illuminating analysis of an extended discussion with Mrs Carpenter and other teachers at Mapledene. They highlight
inadequacies and ambiguities of the accounting vocabulary and also
illustrate the central role of concepts implicitly and explicitly used, such
as 'readiness', 'stages' and 'need' that have recognizable social control
connotations to which the teacher feels she must respond. Not only is the
vocabulary inadequate to explain her curriculum practice, it is also inadequate for her to come to terms with the conflict between the received
and reflexive perspective, a conflict which, at best, remains unresolved.

Conscious of her underlying normative orientations yet devastated by
White when she tries to disown them, unavoidably reinforcing differentia-
tions she is striving to eliminate and handicapped by an accounting vocabulary that obscures rather than illuminates the ambiguities in her position, is there any way in which Miss Sanders may be liberated from the
far-reaching tentacles of the received perspective or is it after all a prison
from which teachers, because they are teachers, may never escape?

Classification and framing

Reassuringly for Miss Sanders, there are areas in which teachers' autonomy may be identified; Bernstein (1971) helps us to identify some of them. He introduces us to two alternative ways of organizing the curriculum in which the development of some opportunities for the exercise of teacher decision making may be glimpsed. He argues that there are two basic types of curriculum organization. It will be useful to consider these at some length if we are to see the implications for curricular decision making. The first is the *collection* type in which the contents are clearly insulated from each other and in which the student has to collect a group of these contents, usually guided by some concept of what the collection is to be used for. The second is a curriculum where the contents are in an open relation to each other – an *integrated* type. Bernstein proceeds to explore these two types of curriculum with the aid of two structural concepts concerning the strength of the boundaries between contents, classification and frame. *Classification* refers to the relationship between contents and the way in which they are differentiated; it is a boundary maintenance concept. *Frame* refers to the relationship between teacher and student; to the strength of the boundary between what may be transmitted and what may not be transmitted in the relationship; its strength determines the degree of control available to the teacher and his students.

Bernstein sees teacher autonomy as being low where classification and framing are strong; here the received model is ascendant. Though he distinguishes between European and English codes of curricular knowledge (educational knowledge codes), Bernstein sees both as being within a received perspective. Curriculum knowledge is presented to the student in a predetermined and hierarchical order to which the teacher is also bound.

Currently the American code with lower classification and framing offers the teacher the possibility of greater autonomy, as indeed it also offers it to the student and the community at large. But in any system autonomy is likely to be even greater when declassification occurs and an integrated curriculum is established. Such integration may involve one or more teachers and be across or within subjects. Integration not only diminishes or eliminates boundaries, it opens up the access to curriculum knowledge by students who may be introduced to basic principles from the beginning as opposed to traditional codes where only an elite group of students could reach these principles after lengthy study. It is at once more public, more democratic and susceptible to debate and decision making in which the teacher can participate rather than 'be on the receiving end'.

Bernstein suggests that there is a strong movement towards the institutionalizing of integrated codes with their characteristic weak classification and framing in both primary and secondary schools. He sees this as offering advances in teacher autonomy as it involves changes in the pattern of work relationships within the school, a weakening boundary between staff and students, more flexible teaching groups, a greater ability 'to tolerate ambiguity both in knowledge and relationships' and 'a pedagogy more concerned with exploring principles than with learning standard operations'. Bernstein sees this change as a challenge to existing social control systems: 'there is a crisis in society's basic classifications and frames, and therefore a crisis in its structures of power and principles of control. . . . This point of view represents an attempt to declassify and so alter power structures and principles of control; in so doing to unfreeze the structure of knowledge and to change the boundaries of consciousness.' Bernstein's arguments and conclusions are closely linked with his concept of a shift from mechanical to organic solidarity enunciated in his paper 'Open Schools — Open Society' (1975). Some of the implications for the teacher and his curriculum organization include:

> In the new schools, integration at the level of idea involves a new principle of social integration of staff: that of organic solidarity. This shift in the basis of the curriculum from subject to idea may point towards a fundamental change in the character of British education: a change from education in depth to education in breadth. . . . There has been a shift from a teaching role which is, so to speak, 'given' (in the sense that one steps into assigned duties), to a role which has to be *achieved* in relation with other teachers. It is a role which is no longer made but *has to be made*.

It is important, however, to notice that Bernstein's analysis is macro cosmic in nature, referring to societies rather than to individual schools or classrooms. In consequence it does not necessarily take into account the variables implicit in the school administration, such as the strong head of department who, by imposing restrictions on the teachers in his department, can turn a curriculum characterized by weak framing into one that is strongly framed. It also takes little account of the potential influence of students which we shall consider in the next chapter. Smith (1976) suggests that students may exercise a powerful influence in moving integrated codes back to a new *egalitarian collection* form as their competitiveness asserts itself.

Curriculum decision making

Taken together, Bernstein's analysis opens up a prospect of a teacher's role in an integrated code that offers a degree of effective professional autonomy that has eluded Miss Sanders in her exploration of the reflexive perspective. Yet it is important to realize that it is a prospect that takes into account not only her interpretation of the curriculum but also the objective realities of curriculum structure and organizations. In short, Bernstein is presenting a prospect of professional decision making that arises in the conditions we have identified as constituting a restructuring perspective.

We may now consider how such a restructuring perspective may be used to identify the parameters of the teacher's role in curriculum; the extent to which the consciousness of the teacher and the structure of the curriculum interrelate to define the content, distribution and evaluation of the curriculum knowledge he uses. In so doing we shall be able to throw further light on the restructuring perspective as well as the received and reflexive perspectives. A convenient starting point is to look at the decisions actually made by all teachers in their day-to-day work in the curriculum.

In order to consider how teachers exercise such decisions in ordering their curricula, it is useful to hypothesize at least four 'curriculum variables' that, in a manner somewhat similar to the Parsonian 'pattern variables', each indicate two theoretically exclusive alternatives. Though it is not suggested that one or other must be chosen by an individual before he can make curriculum decisions, it may be claimed that the variables represent some of the basic dilemmas that are faced by the teacher in considering his curriculum. (In practice most educators achieve a compromise position somewhere on the continua that link the polarities.)

Our four variables of curriculum decisions may be set out as:[2]

1 Traditional/futuristic decisions;
2 Determined/innovatory decisions;
3 Commitment-based/contract-based decisions;
4 Consequential/causal decisions.

A brief description of these variables follows; it is important to remember that, like the received and reflexive perspectives, they are models and are used only as aids to classification and analysis.

1 Traditional/futuristic decisions

On the traditional side of the dichotomy we can see decisions favouring the retention of long-established curriculum patterns. They will involve compulsory training in some subjects of the curriculum and predetermined norms of achievement in the various subjects of a largely unchanging kind. They embrace beliefs that the knowledge, skills and values learned by previous generations have a continuing and major validity in the socialization of the young; that the curriculum possesses a 'mystique' into which the young are initiated and that, when received by those who are chosen to receive it, it will be of continuing relevance throughout their adult lives, even though the 'ultimate truths' may not be revealed until later in life, if at all. Such a curriculum may be claimed to have 'stood the test of time'.

Conversely the futuristic decisions will tend to be hostile to traditional curricula and favourable to new curricula that are believed to be 'relevant' to the expected (different) social conditions in which the young are to be adults. They support curricula based on 'discovery' or 'problem-solving approaches' that embody the view that the future needs of the young will be better served by a developed capacity for 'adaptability' and 'inventiveness' than by remembered knowledge, values and skills. They tend to favour a curriculum that encourages the individuality of the child rather than one that emphasizes his uniformities and embrace a view of a personalized and individual development and a partnership between teacher and students. Curriculum content is seen to be individually achieved rather than collectively ascribed.

Control mediated through these relationships rather than through the ritualistic devices of the traditional curriculum is favoured. Simply, the distinction between the traditional and futuristic decisions may often be seen as one between 'culture taking' and 'culture making'. It is sometimes expressed as one between learning and understanding; certainly most futuristic curricula emphasize individual understanding rather more strongly than learning. There are links between the dichotomy and the Durkheimian concepts of societies based on mechanistic and organic solidarity; the one based on a structure of established and relatively unchanging roles, to which the individual is ascribed; the other on a dynamic structure of individually achieved roles.

2 Determined/innovatory decisions

The determined/innovatory dichotomy is closely linked with the preceding pair, but relates to decisions on organizational arrangements rather than to functional aspirations. On the determined side of the dichotomy are attitudes favouring a curriculum comprising separate elements falling into place in 'coherent' and 'rational' forms with traditional subject divisions and contents, usually involving strong classification and sharply defined hierarchies of subject. Some subjects will be seen to contain high-status knowledge, others the converse. The curriculum tends to comprise subject components each being legitimated by the nature of its 'discipline'or its identifiable area of knowledge.

The behaviour and status of both staff and pupils tends to be dominated by subject specialization and by their ability to perform within the specialist subject. It involves a view of the nature and accessibility of societal knowledge that tends to be both structured and hierarchical.

The determined orientation can also be defined in terms of the concept of boundary maintenance as applied by Bernstein, in that the contents of the separate subjects would be marked off from each other by strong classification. Similarly the teaching method would be marked by strong 'framing', where both teachers and pupils have few, if any, options.

The innovatory side of the dichotomy involves support for the 'flexible school'; there is likely to be support for curricula that are 'integrated' rather than subject based, integration being determined as much by the needs of the individual pupils as by the 'logical grammar' of the subject. In general there is support for flexible school conditions that may be set up in an attempt to achieve objectives such as maximum opportunity for the development of individual pupils and students or to allow for special considerations for their social background and other personal variables. It is essentially 'child-centred' or 'interest-centred' rather than 'subject-centred' education.

The traditional pattern of written examinations appropriate to determined curricula is much less appropriate to the individualized and incompletely predictable outcomes of innovatory curricula and presents difficult if not insoluble problems if the *imprimatur* of the examination boards is still required. Innovatory curricula may be distinguished into two forms, *structured* and *opportunist*. The structured form may be seen in the planned innovatory strategies that characterize the work of many teachers involved in organized programmes to develop innovating curricula in national and local projects, usually with local education authority support. Conversely the opportunist form, however carefully considered, is likely to be of unplanned and unpredictable nature. Spontaneity of child and teacher are terms frequently used by its advocates. The Goldsmiths' Curriculum Laboratory work has many of the characteristics of the opportunist form and, as Musgrove has observed (1964), this may also embody important anti-authoritarian elements.

It is important to separate opportunist innovatory behaviour from the organized and largely predictable progressivism which characterizes many 'progressive' educationalists. Opportunism is characterized by a curriculum that is not fully institutionalized. The existence of the opportunist orientation is manifested by the occurrence of new and not yet fully institutionalized patterns of curriculum decisions. To use Bernstein's terms again, it is likely to be characterized by both weak classification of content and weak framing of pedagogy. Any 'brand' of opportunism is likely to be a transient form in that it becomes institutionalized if it is regarded as successful. And indeed, any form of innovatory curriculum is likely to become, in time, determined through the development of textbooks and materials packages (particularly those regarded as 'teacher proof'), examinations and 'specialists'.

3 Commitment-based/contract-based decisions

Decisions favouring a commitment basis are likely to see the curriculum as a 'total experience' wherein the student is not only involved in a straightforward learning experience but also in a necessary and unavoidable internalization of the official values of the school or college. Curriculum is seen to represent an ideal value system that embodies that which is appropriate or desirable for the adult society. For the students, working through the curriculum is not only a learning situation but also an initiating commitment to an approved societal value system. An important element of the commitment-based orientation is that no part of the curriculum is seen to be legitimately available to the student without the value commitment. Thus the student who renounces the official value orientations of the university may be seen to have no place there and is denied access to any part of its curriculum; the working-class schoolchild has to be converted to not only the knowledge content of the curriculum but also the values of the middle-class school if there is to be 'any point in his education' and he may well be discouraged from staying if his conversion is incomplete. In such situations the reward system of the school as a whole is fully incorporated into the curriculum.

Contract-based decisions involve attitudes that see participation in the curriculum as a contractual arrangement in which students and teachers negotiate arrangements that are limited in their consequences and are usually for some specific rather than general purpose (to pass an examination, to learn a language, etc.). Contractual relationships are more commonly found in community colleges and further education establishments where 'client involvement' has characteristically required direct negotiation between the institution and its students. Elsewhere, notably in universities, it is a position held more commonly by students than by their teachers. An interesting development is the attempt to organize programmes of teaching that specifically exclude moral commitment even though they deal with 'moral issues'. A ready example arises in the Schools Council/Nuffield Humanities Teaching Project where, in the examination of controversial issues such as war, protest and authority, the teacher is explicitly required to encourage pupils to form their own views on these issues rather than to 'receive' those of the teacher or of the school.

In society generally, contractual relationships usually occur between individuals or between organized groups in a structured context. It may be argued that to talk of contractual relationships between individualized students and teachers who form the core of the organization of the school is misleading. Yet the demand for a 'real' contractual relationship is clearly to be seen in a number of current moves, particularly in the upper forms of secondary schools where elective courses and 'consumer choice' schemes are dominant.

4 Consequential orientation/causal decisions

Consequential decisions are likely to view the curriculum as a by-product of other social factors, including the normative and social structure (notably the class and occupational structure) and technological, economic and ideological change. They may support the view that little can be changed by education and that the programmes of social and knowledge engineering envisaged by a number of curriculum developers cannot be undertaken by educational strategies if, indeed, they can be undertaken at all (Hurd and Johnson, 1967). The long-term predictability of genetic if not cultural endowment is unchallenged and may be supported by statements as basic and apparently incontrovertible as 'that's life' or 'he was born that way'.

Causal decision making is likely to view education, at least to some extent, as a determining factor in social behaviour and social organization.

Thus social consequences may be expected to spring from the introduction of educational priority programmes designed to meet the needs of 'deprived' students; social as well as technological consequences may be expected from the introduction of a development programme such as project technology. The roles of teachers and students are seen to allow open if not unlimited prospects of achievement and development, they and their consequences can be 'self-generated'. Evidence such as that published by Douglas (1964) or Rosenthal and Jacobson (1968) that suggests a high degree of child responsiveness to change in the cultural and social environment is likely to be used enthusiastically.

It is now suggested that the four paired variables may be put together as components of a model built around the idea of *autonomy* of the teacher in curriculum decisions. In its simplest form the model would have two extreme identities that may be seen to have a degree of correspondence with Vaughan and Archer's (1971) ideological models of *domination* and *assertion*. Even more clearly they display, respectively, the central characteristics of the received and the reflexive perspectives

(i) where there is no autonomy in curriculum decision making; where the teachers have no significant areas of decision or discretion and are merely agents of a given structure and ideology;

(ii) where curriculum decisions may be wholly autonomous; where the teachers are free to assert their own arrangements without hindrance from a given structure and ideology.

But as we have seen in our consideration of the variables, reality is likely to involve elements of all variables. No curriculum totally ignores the contributions of inspired opportunism. No subject-oriented curriculum completely eliminates child-centred work, even if it is largely relegated to hobby periods. And it must also be recognized that important and established positions cut across the dichotomies. Thus 'cultural education' may call for some highly traditional behaviours yet an associated emphasis on individual expressive work.

Yet, despite the imprecise nature of reality, it is suggested that curriculum decisions are tending to shift from a position nearer (i) to a position nearer (ii). It is further suggested that this has been associated with a shift from a consensus of decision making that has been predominantly associated with those on the left-hand side of each of the four pairs of variables, traditional, determined, commitment-based and consequential. The movement away from such a consensus of decision making is, it is suggested, associated with the four right-hand variables, futuristic, innovatory, contract-based and causal.

Yet the extent to which teachers are able to move away from the left-hand variables characterized by the received perspective is clearly limited, not only by the extent of their enthusiasm for the reflexive perspective but also by the extent of the structured and organization change that is arguable in the school situation. The analysis of curriculum decision making has confirmed the central position of the restructuring perspective as a model of curriculum reality. In the light of the restructuring perspective we have identified areas in the school system where, as a result of the availability of a range of alternative decisions, the possibility of taking autonomous positions on curriculum exists for teachers: moreover we have suggested that some of these areas of decision making may themselves become restructured. The consequences of these possibilities have been noted by many writers with reaction ranging from ecstasy to alarm. Musgrove and Taylor (1969) claim that there is now 'a new despotism: the rule of the teachers' who decide 'what kind of human beings to produce' and argue that teachers' decisions on curriculum content cannot be justified in contemporary society.

Yet the considerations assembled in this chapter still offer little confirmation that teachers are actually using the possibility of autonomy in curriculum in any extensive way; there are no clear indications that the majority of teachers are endeavouring to change the definition, evaluation or distribution of knowledge, still less to modify 'the distribution of power and the principles of social control'. Changes that are occurring in the social structure of modern societies only infrequently seem to spring from within the school curriculum. Teachers' power in curriculum decisions commonly seems to be exercised to reinforce consensus orientations in society rather than to challenge them. Whilst like Miss Sanders they may indeed be surrounded by constraints that lead them to do so, these constraints are reinforced by the teacher's view of his own position in the social structure and his support for social consensus and stability that leads him to use his power in this way and moreover to encourage any potentially deviant colleagues to do so too.

Social control through the curriculum unquestionably exists but often it is of a kind that is embraced by rather than imposed upon the teachers' organization of curriculum in the schools. Yet even though the 'new despotism' in curriculum is used traditionally and usually benignly and not despotically, there is little doubt that teachers in a restructuring context have achieved a position of potential power in curriculum. It is possible that we are only just beginning to glimpse some of the complications for social control that may accrue from this.

Students and the curriculum

In previous chapters we have emphasized the role of teachers in the curriculum. This is not surprising. Though teachers are markedly out-numbered by the young in every school, they regularly display a dis-proportionate sensitivity to the behaviour of other teachers. This was early noted by Waller (1932):

> The significant people for a school teacher are other teachers, and by comparison with good standing in that fraternity the good opinion of students is a small thing and of little price. A landmark in one's assimilation to the profession is that moment when he decides that only teachers are important.

But if we are to consider the sociology of the curriculum fully we must now pay attention to the other important partners in the process. In British schools and most others they are still regularly called pupils − a term which unambiguously denotes the lower status to which they are ascribed. But the increasing use of the label 'student', previously reserved for those at college and university, may be seen to mark a greater recognition of their participation in curriculum processes.

Student 'power'

Certainly there has been some development of the idea that children may play a part in determining their curriculum. In the recent past the opportunity for pupils to exercise 'power' was restricted to the incor-poration of a small group of senior pupils into a suitably lowly position in the teacher group − as monitors or prefects, where their task was essentially to ensure that the teachers' curriculum decisions were re-inforced and supported by a suitably limited range of disciplinary strategies. But apart from this tightly controlled and limited opportunity, the role of the pupil was essentially a recipient one and children quickly came to realize that the teacher's question 'What shall we do today then?' was strictly rhetorical and only to be answered at risk.

But in the modern primary school, theories of child-centred education have, as we have seen, led to a situation in which children's expressed interests appear to be used to determine what the content of the curriculum should be. It is important to remember, however, that it still remains the teachers' task to identify these interests and also the needs of children according to professional criteria that are not, and perhaps cannot be, normally utilized by the children themselves. The examples of teacher behaviour quoted in the previous chapter even suggest that in some situations informal child-centred methods can lead to a diminution of the power of the children to determine the outcomes of the curriculum.

In the secondary school the evidence of pupil decision making is also ambiguous. There project-type activities, including problem-solving approaches in the humanities, technology, literature and other subject areas, appear to take pupil power somewhat farther in that it is the student whose task it is to help to identify the problems, find solutions and evaluate them. In theory the teacher may act as no more than one expert resource amongst many others that the pupil might call upon in a process of discovery, innovation and creative experience. But, in practice, the teacher may do much more than this, exercising considerable influence to ensure that not only the 'right' problems are tackled but also the 'right' answers are achieved. Recently a teacher of applied science, well known for his 'successful' projects, confided 'the secret is to feed-in your own ideas to the kids at the right time and to know when to intervene; you just haven't got time to make mistakes when you've only got three periods a week'.

Yet a further area of curriculum power of the pupils in many schools appears to be the freedom to choose and even to withdraw from some or all of the activities of the curriculum. At the end of compulsory schooling the student has the ultimate power to withdraw totally. Full-time staying on after minimum leaving age is wholly voluntary and its uneven incidence has its own powerful influence on curriculum. But a few schools, such as Countesthorpe in Leicestershire (Bernbaum, 1974), offer, within the school, the opportunity to withdraw from classes. Instead pupils may undertake private study or even leisure activities in the 'youth service area' of the school. Many schools now offer students the opportunity of choosing between a range of option curriculum courses; they may elect to follow combinations of subject areas in their fields of interest — often these have occupational connotations with which students may identify themselves. Schools with such programmes usually have a school counsellor associated with them; the counsellor, a teacher with appropriate training, has the task of helping pupils to make curriculum decisions in the light of their abilities, prospects and interests which he has helped them to identify.

In their most developed form, such counselling schemes come very near to mobilizing student power over the curriculum most fully. The counsellor using his diagnostic and advisory skills in detailed discussions with, say, fourth form students, may well have established a comprehensive list of the curricular requirements of the students preparing for their fifth year of schooling. To what extent is this 'authoritative' list of requirements binding? Let us imagine that the list shows that there is a substantial demand for commercial courses with typewriting, book-keeping and other applied activities and that this arises in a comprehensive school that has recently been translated from a grammar school with a long tradition and a heavy investment in the teaching of classics and the arts. What is the outcome likely to be? Does the school invest its money in typewriters and accounting machines and cancel its order for the new texts of the Cambridge Latin project? In practice the answer varies, as might be expected, in accordance with the staff and the ideologies they hold. They range from a steadfast refusal to abandon 'true academic standards in favour of fashion' to a willingness to modify staffing appointment and deployment policies in a way that 'facilitates the needs of the students'.

In practice, however, most schools effect a compromise in which there are explicit and implicit restrictions on the choices available to students, both between choices and within them. In such circumstances the counsellors may well find themselves with a role that is translated to one of 'selling' the school curricular programmes to the students, convincing them that what the school has available and is prepared to offer them is in fact right for them; a state of affairs that has been described by Cicourel and Kitsuse (1963), in their celebrated account of the affairs of Lakeshore High School where such practices not only occurred but were also clearly recognized by the students.

Does this mean, then, that student power over the curriculum is based upon only slender foundations; that in many schools it is at most superficial and that students are fundamentally only free to conform to a situation that is predetermined? Are the pupils as unfree as the teachers appeared to be in the received perspective we considered in the previous chapter? Does the only possibility for pupils to play an active role in curriculum decisions lie not within the curriculum but, as Holly (1973) has suggested, beyond the curriculum as we presently know it in the school?

The good pupil role

Certainly for most children participating in curriculum means being asked to play the *good pupil* role responding to the definitions, evaluations and distributions of curriculum knowledge administered by and through the teacher. The traditional ingredients of the good pupil role are familiar. They include paying attention to the teacher, working hard, being committed to achieving the rewards offered by the teacher for successful conformity, no copying or showing of work to other pupils other than in specifically authorized situations, the ability to give the right answer or at least to feel suitably dismayed when for whatever reason he is unable to do so. In demeanour the good pupil is interested, enthusiastic, responsive, polite, respectful and desirous of pleasing the teacher. As Sharp and Green (1975) emphasize, 'he will be characterised by his business'. He will be expected to develop according to norms appropriate for his age, sex and social position. He must not be a paragon, however. Calvert (1975) has pointed out that 'he should not get everything right because this would suggest that he hardly needed teaching'. The learning of these norms forms an important part of socialization and is very closely linked with the models of curriculum that we have discussed earlier in the book. Central to the positivist view of the development of children is Piaget (1958), whose categorization of the stages of development through which all normal children will pass is part of the inner core of knowledge transmitted to all teachers in training.

But there are other, reflexive views of the nature of development that emphasize not only diversity but also a relationship with the prior and present condition of the child rather than a general norm. Here the work of Baratz and Baratz (1970) in their study of New York children is illuminating. The work of Bronfenbrenner (1970) indicating the strikingly different 'models of childhood' that are approved and endorsed in different societies also lends support to the relativist argument. And there are, of course, within every school, system variations in the definition of the good role; Miss Sanders, whom we met in

Chapter 5, would probably expect a far higher degree of 'noise' and mobility in her classroom than that which Donat's 'Mr Chips' sought and finally achieved. But there is little doubt that most teachers of whatever persuasion will have in their minds something approaching the vision of Sand (1968) who described the ideal child 'sitting on the edge of his seat, his eyes shining'. Hargreaves (1972) has emphasized how important it is for pupils to behave in these ways; if they do not, teachers are unable to live up to their own conception of their developmental curricular roles.

The negative pupil role

Yet, as we have seen, the nature and availability of curriculum knowledge are not always of a kind to which all students may respond with enthusiasm. In our discussion of social control we have noticed that important areas of the curriculum may have the consequences of making many children realize their inadequacies, conveying to them the personal experience of failure. There are in fact *two* polar categories of pupil role in the curriculum, both of them familiar to all teachers. At the opposite end of the scale from the good pupil role is its corollary, the *negative* pupil role. Here the components are sharply different – those of boredom, frustration, a desire to impede if not to make impossible the teacher's curricular role. To such students, staying on at school longer than is necessary is unthinkable; well before reaching the minimum statutory leaving age they have realized that, for them, the consequences of participating in the curriculum being offered to them carry only the prospect of continuing subservience, deference and low status and commitment to a life of being on the 'receiving end'.

These polar types of student role have been documented in detail in a Schools Council report *Young School Leavers* (1969). The attitudes and responses to school of those who leave at minimum leaving age are shown to be markedly different from those who desire to continue their full-time schooling. Their choice and evaluation of curriculum subjects, their acceptance of the behavioural norms of their school, their perception of their future prospects and the relevance of schooling to them are all fundamentally different. Those who leave early see themselves as having experienced a curriculum that has denied them the opportunity of participation or power in society. They see themselves as having experienced a curriculum that is designed to put them on the 'receiving end' rather than one that has 'contracted them in' to the possibilities of responsible participation in adult society and community.

Making students different

The key process which brings about differentiation of this kind is, predominantly, the differential experience of curriculum. To some a curriculum of high-status knowledge has been offered; to others the reverse. The most visible way in which schools have regularly brought about these differences is through the operation of streaming or 'tracking'. Yet even the abolition of streaming that has now taken place in many schools in no way necessarily modifies the process. Nash (1974) has shown how even in unstreamed school situations not only is different knowledge made available to different students which seems to have different intellectual and social characteristics, but also that the children are fully aware of what is happening.

For an illuminating account of the complex differentiation processes taking place in the curricula of a 'progressive' British primary school we may turn to the research of Sharp and Green (1975) at Mapledene School. Here we may see the way in which the teachers' perspectives allow them to identify and categorize the various good pupil roles to certain children who are labelled as 'really able', 'a bright one' and similar categories. But we may also see the way in which the same perspectives identify the pupils to whom these good roles cannot be attributed. Such children are defined as problems; they are abnormal, odd or peculiar, with labels such as 'just a plodder' and 'really thick'. One example is Michael — an infant about whom Mrs Carpenter reports:

> Nothing I said would make any difference, you know, he wouldn't
> . . . he didn't want to write or anything, he wasn't very interested in
> that. He wasn't very interested in joining in with a reading group —
> he wasn't very interested in the story. He just wanted to go on his
> own sweet way . . . he just dribbed and drabbed about . . . you know,
> he never had a true friend.

In the light of Sharp and Green's analyses, several important points may be made. One is that, in the ethic of the progressive curriculum with its emphases on openness and child centredness, it is unacceptable to talk of negative pupil roles. Yet in the ethic of the teaching profession it is equally unacceptable to suggest that it is the fault of the teacher that a child like Michael has not successfully achieved the good pupil role. Accordingly it is necessary to define the child as deficient in some way to account for his failure in a curriculum that because of its enlightened nature is seen to be right for different individual children. In Michael's case, as in a number of others, his problems are attributed to the deficiencies of home. Thus another teacher, Mrs Lyons, sees her pupils as:

> The products of largely unstable and uncultured backgrounds, with parents who are, in various combinations, irresponsible, incompetent, illiterate, 'clueless', uninterested and unappreciative of education, and who, as a result fail to prepare their children adequately for the experiences they will be offered in school.
>
> The parents, especially the mothers, tend to be spoken of very disparagingly. The mothers are perceived as generally immature and unable to cope, having too many young children either by accident or design whilst they are still too young. The teacher declares that many mothers go to work to help pay off rent arrears and electricity bills incurred through bad management. She castigates them for creating latchkey children and for frittering away their conscience money on toys and unsuitable clothes (hot pants, etc.) in an attempt to relieve 'their guilt' at neglecting them.

The affairs of Mapledene School show us the ways in which the models of the pupil are deeply rooted in the consciousness of the teachers, even in an avowedly child-centred school, and above all how they are imposed on the day-to-day behaviour of the children.

Reification

An illuminating part of Sharp and Green's analysis is the description of the process in which the teacher's expectations of pupils are communicated to the children and the tendency of children to adopt these expectations and act them out.

This spiralling process whereby teacher and child together develop identities that come, in themselves, to determine the curriculum that can be taught by the teacher and responded to by the child is called *reification*. The labels for the good and bad pupil roles become reified not only as teachers' categories but also as individual children's identities. Even in Mapledene where teachers were aware of 'the self-fulfilling prophecy', there was abundant evidence of the process. Thus Mrs Buchanan comments:

In an ideal situation you'd have them all so keen and interested that they'd get on and just come to you for book references and this and that and the other (laughter) but here, they don't seem to get involved in anything, not for any length of time anyway. They've got a very short span of concentration, they've got no perseverance at all. You've got to be standing over them, all the time, pushing them.

A particularly interesting example is the case of the child who breaks through a negative identity to become a good pupil. Sharp and Green present the story of Linda:

The teacher described the mother as 'not cultured' and communicates the view that the family background is not conducive to great success. The mother, for example, did not complete the child's medical form so she missed seeing the doctor, and she had 'pushed the child onto an older brother' to bring to school after the first day — both were taken to be indications of general neglect. . . . Three weeks later, however, the picture had changed. The child was now a success story. The headmaster was heard to remark that he thought her a real problem child when she first came but she 'conforms now reasonably' and the teacher also said she was 'potentially odd but bright enough to conform'.

. . . What happened to explain Linda's transformation? The teacher denied any responsibility for the change. 'Linda did it all herself — she transformed herself'. Such a view is, of course, in line with the child centred faith in the spontaneous development of the child itself. The teacher denied that she had given the child 'special' treatment. Nevertheless, the observer noting the teacher's avowal that the child needed 'sitting on' remarked that the child received more than usual instruction in the type of behaviour expected. Unlike some other new children, she was being singled out for individual instruction, for example in learning to say 'please' to Mrs Lyons' 'excuse me'. She was clearly being told how to behave. Moreover, in spite of her 'bizarre' behaviour she soon appeared to have sufficient powers of concentration to pursue a task through to the end, she 'knew her colours' and could count and seemed to understand the teacher's instructions and comply with them. Furthermore, she was able to gear into the teacher's system of relevancies very quickly.

. . . It seems that the key to the child's transformed identity lies in the fact that the teacher did differentiate her treatment towards this child in a way which brought about a closer approximation to the ideal pupil.

In the concept of reification we have yet another example of the constraints that impede the exercise of an autonomous role by teachers and by students. Yet they are constraints that, for the most part, spring from within the teacher or the student. Unquestionably such constraints are not the avowed intention of the teachers, rather it is the practice of reflexive and progressive education that reinforces the very differentiation of pupils that they are trying to counter.

Student roles in the secondary school

The even sharper polarization that takes place during the experience of the secondary school curriculum after the formative experiences of the primary curriculum has been diagnosed by Hargreaves (1967) in a well-known study of a British streamed secondary modern school. He writes:

> Those with positive orientations towards the values of the school will tend over the four years to converge on the higher streams; and those with negative orientations will tend to converge on the lower streams. On every occasion that a boy is 'promoted' or 'demoted' on the basis of school examination, the greater becomes a concentration of the two opposing subcultures. . . . For boys in high streams life at school will be a pleasant and rewarding experience, since the school system confers status upon them. This status is derived from membership of a high stream, where boys are considered to be academically successful, and are granted privileges and responsibility in appointment as prefects and in their selection for school visits and holidays. The peer-group values reflect the status bestowed on such boys by the school in being consonant with teachers' values. Conformity to peer-group and school values is thus consistent and rewarding.
>
> In the low streams boys are deprived of status, in that they are *double failures* by their lack of ability or motivation to obtain entry to a Grammar School or to a high stream in the Modern School. The school, as we have seen, accentuates this state of failure and deprivation. The boys have achieved virtually nothing. For boys in low streams conformity to teacher expectations gives little status. We can thus regard the low-stream boys as subject to status frustration, for not only are they unable to gain any sense of equality of worth in

the eyes of the school, but their occupational aspirations for their future lives in society are seriously reduced in scope. . . . Demotion to the delinquescent subculture is unlikely to encourage a boy to strive towards academic goals, since the pressures within the peer group will confirm and reinforce the anti-academic attitudes which led to demotion, and the climate within the low streams will be far from conducive to academic striving. In order to obtain promotion from a low stream, a boy must deviate from the dominant anti-academic values. . . .

In many secondary schools the process seems to be an almost inescapable one, yet one that is based almost wholly upon the curriculum ideology adopted and transmitted by the staff, augmented by a range of associated beliefs about the necessity of restriction of entry to examinations, about the limited range of opportunity seen to be available in continued education and, fundamentally, the limited availability of rewards within society. But above all the conflict is reinforced by the pupils themselves, whose value orientations become increasingly divergent, who reinforce the segregation within the curriculum by an increasing separation in leisure activities, so that they eventually come to have very real fears of the prospect of demotion or promotion to an alien sub-culture of students with whom they have little or nothing in common. By the final year the lower-stream pupils have developed a status-satisfaction system of their own by establishing what Hargreaves has called the *delinquescent subculture* both within and outside the school. Yet like the curricula of the lower-stream pupils, it is one that anticipates an adult role that is seen as inferior by the school.

Hargreaves's saga of 'Lumley School' is particularly vivid in his account of the C and B stream students who in their delinquescent subculture find ever-increasing ways of impeding the teacher in his curricular role and preoccupying him with his difficult, even overwhelming, disciplinary role. Such strategies included in the growing of hair always at a greater length than that which the teacher is prepared to tolerate; the wearing of light blue jeans when the teacher has conceded to the wearing of dark blue jeans; the use of bovver boots and platform soles. The list is infinite; the confrontation almost inevitable, as Goffman (1971) shows in his description of the complex subtleties of *body gloss* — the way in which people use posture, distance and bodily and facial expressions to express their feelings about their situation. In the school non-verbal expression is often favoured; its ambiguous message can be denied if the teacher challenges the student (or vice versa) about its offensive nature. 'Acting cool' is typical, as Goffman describes:

> But of all the techniques used by gang members to communicate rejection of authority, by far the most subtle and annoying to teachers is demeanour. Both white and Negro gang members have developed a uniform and highly stylised complex of body movements that communicate a casual and disdainful aloofness to anyone making normative claims on their behaviour. The complex is referred to by gang members as 'looking cool'. . . . The essential ingredients of 'looking cool' are a walking pace that is a little too slow for the occasion, a straight back, shoulders slightly stooped, hands in pockets, and eyes that carefully avert any party to the interaction. There are also clothing aides which enhance the effect such as boot or shoe taps and a hat if the scene takes place indoors. It is the teacher who must make the first move. Teachers do not miss it but they have great difficulty in finding anything to attack.

The hidden curriculum

Is then the role of the student in curriculum confined to playing either the good pupil role with varying degrees of enthusiasm or the negative pupil role with varying degrees of hostility? Such an analysis is still far too crude to explain the subtlety of the relationships between teacher and student through which the curriculum is negotiated. To take matters farther we must look more fully at the *hidden curriculum* which was first mentioned in Chapter 2 and of which the shared identities of Mapledene, the delinquescent sub-cultures of Hargreaves and the gang behaviours of Goffman are but components. Jackson (1968) in his *Life in Classrooms* drew attention to this unofficial curriculum. He saw it as a

> . . . hidden curriculum which each student (and teacher) must master if he is to make his way satisfactorily through the school. The demands created by these features of classroom life may be contrasted with the academic demands – the 'official' curriculum, so to speak – to which educators have traditionally paid most attention. As might be expected, the two curriculums are related to each other in several important ways. . . . Indeed, many of the rewards and punishments that sound as if they are being dispensed on the basis of academic success and failure are really more closely related to the mastery of the hidden curriculum.

Jackson argues that every child and every teacher has to learn this essential curriculum if he is to survive in the classroom and even to begin to participate in the official curriculum. The concept is important not only for the revelation of previously unrecognized components of curriculum in the classrooms but also because it alerts us to previously unrecognized ways in which the student plays an important part, at times even the major part in defining, evaluating and distributing knowledge. Here we come closer to the heart of the elusive identification of the exercise of pupil power in the classroom.

To recognize the hidden curriculum more clearly we may, with some assistance from Jackson, draw up a list of components that will at once alert every reader with experience of the classroom to its central determining role in day-to-day curricular activities. It is of course impossible to compile a complete list but some of the central items will be:

1   Learning to 'live in crowds', involving the postponement or even the denial of personal desires such as talking to a teacher who is already dealing with somebody else; the ability to tolerate or to ignore interruption and disturbance; the capacity to wait an hour for the purple paint or even a week for the wood saw or drill because others are using them at a time when one urgently desires to use them oneself.

2   Closely associated with 1 is learning to use or to lose time, tolerating boredom and passivity as an inevitable component of being in the classroom. Jackson writes:

> The quintessence of virtue in most institutions is contained in the single word: *patience*. Lacking that quality, life could be miserable for those who must spend their time in our prisons, our factories, our corporation offices, and our schools. In all of these settings, the participants must learn to labour and to wait. They must also, to some extent, learn to suffer in silence.

3   Learning to accept assessment by others; not only by teachers but also by fellow pupils. Again Jackson elaborates the point:

> Every child experiences the pain of failure and the joy of success long before he reaches school age, but his achievements, or lack of them, do not really become official until he enters the classroom. From then on, however, a semi-public record of his progress gradually accumulates, and as a student he must learn to adapt to the continued and pervasive spirit of evaluation that will dominate his school years. *Evaluation*, then, is another important fact of life in the elementary classroom.

But evaluation is also a product of the peer group, as the experiences described by Lacey (1970) in his account of Hightown Grammar School make clear:

> When I first started observing the first-year classes in March 1963, the members of each class had been together for only about six months, but each class already had a definite structure of which pupils clearly had a detailed knowledge. When a master called a boy to read or answer a question, others could be seen giving each other significant looks which clearly indicated that they knew what to expect. On one occasion, for example, a master asked three boys to stay behind after the lesson to help him with a task calling for a sense of responsibility and co-operation. He called out 'Williams, Maun and Sherring'. The class burst into spontaneous laughter, and there were unbelieving cries of 'What! Sherring?' The master corrected himself. 'No, not Sherring, Shadwell.' From the context of the incident it was clear that Sherring's reputation was already inconsistent with the qualities expected of a monitor.

4   Learning how to compete to please both teachers and fellow students in order to obtain their praise, reward and esteem by appropriate behaviours. This also involves attracting attention to these behaviours and on occasions a capacity to forgo the rewards for other desired personal advantages. As Henry (1960) puts it, 'What the child learns is how to give an acceptable performance'. Every child in every schoolroom has to know how to give teacher what he wants, every teacher has to frame wants that are not only satisfying to his students but which also embody sufficient clues for children to be able to identify clearly what is wanted.

5   Learning how to live in a hierarchical society and to be differentiated in the process. Parsons (1961) has drawn attention to the way in which a relatively non-stratified school intake is translated into a stratified group with close parallels to the stratification system of the outside world. Jackson draws attention to this part of the hidden curriculum in the process:

> The fact of unequal power is a third feature of classroom life to which students must become accustomed. The difference in authority between the teacher and his students is related, quite obviously, to the evaluative aspects of classroom life. But it involves much more than the distribution of praise and reproof. This difference provides the most salient feature of the social structure of the classroom and

its consequences relate to the broader conditions of freedom, privilege, and responsibility as manifest in classroom affairs.

Developing a capacity to live with and to tolerate social differentiation is a widely evident consequence of the hidden curriculum. It is well-known that in most school systems students may complain with some bitterness about the injustices of their fellows who hold higher-status roles such as 'prefect' or 'captain' or 'monitor'. Yet rarely, if at all, do they complain about the *existence* of such roles; the hidden curriculum has taught them to accept them. Students regularly come to have a clear view of the social structure and of their own position in it and frequently differentiate themselves sharply from their fellows in different positions with remarks such as 'I wouldn't join that bunch of stuck-up snobs' or conversely 'I couldn't bear going with that group of deadbeats'.

6   With one's fellow students, learning ways to control the speed and progress of what the teacher presents in the official curriculum. Classrooms abound with skilful devices where, through distracting teachers with diversionary questioning, bogus claims that familiar material is in fact unfamiliar and difficult, the losing of pens and pencils and a thousand other delaying strategies, students are able to exercise substantial control over the speed with which they are required to work.

7   The learning of shared meanings with the aid of an established shorthand or restricted code of language. Such learning facilitates the operation of the other aspects of the hidden curriculum, allowing teachers and students to affirm to each other that they know and understand the procedures in which they are both involved. A typical example is that of the English teacher who wished to remind his class that words of identical spelling can in fact have different meanings. Having achieved the meanings of the word 'chest' as a piece of furniture for storage and as part of the body, he then sought to show the risk of ambiguity of such a word, putting it into a sentence as 'He opened the window and threw out his chest'. The humour that could arise from a confusion between the two meanings in such a sentence was not lost on the class. The teacher followed this with a practical demonstration which clearly lived in the minds of his class; for weeks afterwards, when a student was called upon to open the window there was a murmur of 'and throw out his chest' throughout the class. The teacher, alert to this implication, translated his instruction, when ventilation was next needed, by asking a child to 'throw out his chest'. The

meaning was immediately perceived by the class and became part of the shared consciousness of the teacher and students.

But as Dreeben (1967) has made clear the underlying purpose of the hidden curriculum, as with the official curriculum, is to learn the norms that are of relevance to society. He writes:

> Four norms have particular relevance to economic and political participation in industrial societies; those of independence, achievement, universalism, and specificity. I have selected these, not because they form an exhaustive list, but because they are central to the dominant, non-familial activities of adults in American society. In school, pupils participate in activities where they are expected to act as if they were conforming to these norms whether they actually accept them at a particular time or not. Through such participation, it is my belief, pupils will in time know their content, accept them as binding upon themselves, and act in accordance with them in appropriate situations.

Learning the hidden curriculum

The hidden curriculum is not new. Vallance (1973) has undertaken an interesting study of the hidden curriculum to be seen in nineteenth-century educational reform, interpreting the language of 'justification' used in educational argument and debate. Because the hidden curriculum is a longstanding and widely recognized part of the culture of our society, its learning may be anticipated by children even before schooling begins. Indeed to watch pre-school children playing 'schools' provides a ready guide to some of the more recurring component elements of the hidden curriculum. By the time he reaches school every child brings with him a rudimentary knowledge of the roles he is expected to play. Moreover he has a remarkably detailed knowledge of the standard characteristics and roles of teachers. The writer remembers vividly an occasion when his 3-year-old son was looking at some promotional leaflets issued by a mail-order book company. The books being advertised were a new edition of Churchill's war memoirs. The leaflets were illustrated by a picture of Churchill in aggressive mood printed in black on a red background. The child who at that time had had no personal contact with schools whatsoever took one look, turned around and said, 'Daddy, it's a headmaster'.

For the new pupil arriving in an established class, the learning of the hidden curriculum becomes an urgent necessity, preceding any hope of effective participation in the official curriculum. Where shall he sit and how? What fine balance of attention or indifference is tolerable both to the teacher and to his classmates? How fully can he respond to the teacher's questioning? With what vocabulary and what intonation may he talk to the teacher? What are the expectations of the teacher concerning talking in class, performance of written work, honesty of marking? Which of his fellow pupils and teachers must he learn to respect and tolerate; which must he learn to distrust and not to tolerate? The hidden curriculum, like the official curriculum, is vast, detailed and complex. But unlike the official curriculum the sanctions that enforce it are usually inexorable and virtually inescapable. Much the same may be said for the new teacher in an established day. He, too, has to be keenly sensitive, as Geer (1968) reminds us:

> By listening carefully to what a teacher says he wants in class and comparing among themselves what grades or comments he gives for what kinds of work, and by 'trying things on' . . . in the early days of a school term, a class may reach a consensus about a teacher's standards, both academic and disciplinary. It then transforms what the teacher says and does into rules for him to follow. He must not change the rules the class makes for him, and he must apply them to all pupils.

But the process of mutual exploration between teachers and pupils over curriculum roles is continuous, as Holt (1964, p. 114) makes clear:

> Atlas Paper II asks the student, 'What two key words on each index page of the Atlas tell at a glance which names can be found on that page?' . . . The other day Abby and Jane could not understand what the instructions were asking them to do, largely because they were too busy thinking about the answer to be able to think about the instructions. We studied the examples given in the paper, but to no avail. Finally, I told them to sit at their desks and think about it some more. A minute or two later Jane appeared at the door and said indignantly, 'Are you *sure* that it isn't those two words at the top of the page?' Having said no such thing, I was taken aback, and said with some surprise, 'When did I say that?' She immediately turned to Abby, who was waiting outside the door, and said 'Write it down!' She had all the clues she needed.

Certainly the hidden curriculum is essential learning for both student and teacher. Without it the working of the official curriculum would collapse. Consider for instance the work of the mathematics teacher. In the official curriculum he will often emphasize the importance of individual work and the negative aspects of cheating or other collaborative activities when his students are called upon to solve problems. Yet every teacher of mathematics knows that collaboration to find the correct answers is widespread and that were this not the case the volume of wrong answers that he would be called upon to correct would be so vast that his marking and assessment systems would almost certainly break down. For him cheating and collaboration are essential if the official curriculum is to continue. Occasionally he may recognize the dissonance that is mutually tolerated by telling a child who has been caught in particularly flagrant circumstances, 'You shouldn't have been so stupid as to get caught'.

Much the same is true in science. Experimental work is an essential characteristic of most science teaching, yet every teacher knows that when students are performing experiments the number of variables that can cause the experiment to fail are many. Yet if the learning experience that is believed to be associated with obtaining the correct result is to be achieved, some assistance in 'fixing' the experiments so that, within the lesson period, most students achieve correct results, is needed. Here the laboratory technician is a key figure helping students to 'get it right' with new material and occasionally with supplies of the finished product. He works busily in the laboratory in full view of the teacher and yet is apparently invisible to him.

The laboratory is also used as an example by Delamont (1976), where Miss Linnaeus is teaching. Miss Linnaeus is teaching the effect of light on the leaves of plants. The experiment involves partial covering of the leaves with foil in order to exclude light. One of her more perceptive students asks if Miss Linnaeus can be sure that the ensuing differences in the colour of the leaf can be wholly attributed to the effect of the foil. Miss Linnaeus, deeply committed to inquiry methods in science teaching, is faced with a dilemma. The question, if it is to be adequately answered, will delay the lesson and take her whole attention from the rest of the class. Another pupil, equally perceptive but this time more sensitive to the hidden curriculum, interrupts to say that of course it works in the expected way because they wouldn't be doing the experiment were it otherwise. In such brief moments of truth the unresolved juxtaposition of the two curricula may be publicly recognized in the classroom.

The hidden curriculum and social control

The inconvenience and even embarrassment of such a moment indicates one of the reasons why the hidden curriculum is hidden. Another reason springs from its central importance in the operation of the control system in the classroom. One of the conventions of the teaching profession, at least until recently, has been that while discussion of the curriculum may be public that of class control may not be. For the good teacher control is supposed to be effortless, springing from superior personal qualities that should be present in any teacher. Those who talk of control may risk implying that in some way they lack the necessary attributes. To find a detailed account of control and its problems we have to turn, not to real-life accounts, but to fiction (for example, Blishen, 1966).

Teachers' reticence may give the less reticent students some advantages in the exercise of influence through the hidden curriculum. But the student may also hold influence because ultimately his superior bargaining power is unanswerable. In the last resort he has control over the essential productivity of the classroom, that of learning, by withdrawing his labour or at least by 'working to rule'. But for the most part hidden curriculum appears to spring from negotiation between teachers and taught. At Wabash High School, well known in the sociological literature, the school administration was seen to have a keen desire for a well-ordered institution yet did not call for close supervision of the grading system. In consequence there developed, through the hidden curriculum, a well-worked-out trading system whereby teachers and pupils traded good grades for orderly performance. Rist (1970), in his study of ghetto schools, drew attention to the sophisticated collusion between the undemanding regime of teachers that allowed students to get by with low performance in return for which the students did not challenge the teacher's low profile of expectation — a mutually self-fulfilling treaty.

The hidden curriculum not only facilitates agreed production strategies, it protects both teachers and students from excess demands of each other. In short, it facilitates and contains the official curriculum by establishing the dialectic of the classroom. As Jackson reminds us:

> The reward system of the school is linked to success in both curriculums. Indeed, many of the rewards and punishments that sound as if they are being dispensed on the basis of academic success and

failure are really more closely related to the mastery of the hidden curriculum. Consider, as an instance, the common teaching practice of giving a student credit for trying. What do teachers mean when they say a student tries to do his work? They mean, in essence, that he complies with the procedural expectations of the institution. He does his homework (though incorrectly), he raises his hand during class discussion (though he doesn't turn the page very often). He is, in other words, a 'model' student, though not necessarily a good one.

Teacher perspectives and student perspectives

We have now reached the point where the distinction between the hidden curriculum and the official curriculum may be discarded. What we are seeing is in fact two perspectives on the total curriculum — the official curriculum that is predominantly a teacher perspective and the hidden curriculum that is predominantly a student perspective. But the device has alerted us to notice what is otherwise obscure: that the pupil has, through the informal culture of the school, a real influence on the way things are — an influence that appears far greater than that envisaged in recent 'official' strategies to give him 'power' through option courses, projects and the like. Essentially the hidden curriculum, in showing the dynamic links between the consciousness of the students and the structural realities of the school and its curriculum, offers further corroboration of the potential of the restructuring perspective set out in Chapter 4 of this volume.

Yet, though the hidden curriculum holds out the prospect of student power in the curriculum, our account suggests that for the most part it acts as one with the official curriculum as an agent of social control. It identifies the students with 'their place' in the social system, brings them into compliance with its norms and values and with the structures and the sanctions with which they are imposed. The curriculum becomes even more clearly identified as being not just about subjects or even examinations but about a way of life. It is certainly arguable that, within this way of life for most students, it is the hidden curriculum components rather than the official subject components that have enduring existence — possibly because, though hidden, they are more effectively taught. The prospect of student power, though implicit throughout the hidden curriculum, seems to be as constrained as the teacher power we explored in the previous chapter. In practice, in all types of school, both appear to offer no more than a power to conform.

As Smith (1976) has suggested, one of the most likely uses of student power is to move integrated curricula back to a position of egalitarian collection with a student- rather than a teacher-induced competitive ethic.

Summary

An exploration of the student role in the curriculum was commenced with a consideration of student 'power'. This led to consideration of the curriculum roles available to students and the ways in which they differentiate students along teacher-oriented lines through such processes as reification. But a more effective possibility of student power was seen to lie within the hidden curriculum which was analysed in detail as an important guide to the practice of curriculum in the classroom. Yet the analysis suggests that the hidden curriculum is as one with the official curriculum as an instrument of social control in which students, like teachers, have for the most part only the power to conform.

The sociology of curriculum development

Underlying all the ideological debates and the interplay of teacher and student roles outlined in the previous chapters has been the process of curriculum change. The process is a continuing one; an inevitable corollary of technical, economic and social change. The curriculum in mathematics changes in the face of computerization; the science curriculum responds to an age of nuclear physics; language changes with the advent of new media of communication. But change in the knowledge content of the curriculum opens up the prospect of change in the nature of social control; the process of adjustment loosens the established pattern of the definition, distribution and evaluation of knowledge, however momentarily, to new or existing groups who seek to make it more responsive to their views and their conditions. Such opportunities have repeatedly occurred within societies and we have seen some of the ensuing political consequences in Chapter 3 of this volume. In the independent progressive schools the incidence of curriculum change has been strikingly visible, as Stewart (1972) has documented. But even within the state school systems the increasing speed of technological, economic and social change in the second half of the present century has led to a markedly increased incidence of change in curriculum content.

But an even more important development since the closing years of the 1950s has been the concept of *planned curriculum change* – the attempt to impose a rational order on a previously spasmodic and often unordered process of updating knowledge. Centuries of predominantly unplanned change were followed by 'a new certainty that all aspects of curriculum were susceptible to planning' (Mackenzie, 1964). Many reasons have been advanced for this dramatic change of emphasis. A widespread belief in the desirability of a planned social system that could alleviate if not eliminate the handicaps and hardships of social

119

and economic inequality arose in most Western societies in the late 1950s. It involved in particular a belief that suitable changes in our educational arrangements could be used to bring about desired social changes; many arguments implied that a redistribution of educational opportunity could in itself change the class structure unaided by other instruments. Curricular change not only in content but also in methodology came to be seen as an important component of social engineering through education. Thinking of this nature was augmented from a different and unexpected source after the successful Russian launching of the Sputnik spacecraft. It was claimed that Western societies were technologically disadvantaged and a popular solution was seen to lie in curriculum reforms that introduced a heavier and more effective emphasis on science and technology into the schools.

Diffuse initiatives of these kinds were utilized and brought into sharper focus by a number of bodies on both sides of the Atlantic. In Britain the most notable pioneering work was undertaken by the Nuffield Foundation in the science subjects. Largely based upon the work of the Science Masters Association (later with the Association of Women Science Teachers forming the Association of Science Education), this opened up a new wave of rational curriculum development. In these new Nuffield approaches the *objectives* of the curriculum were diagnosed and formulated, the *methodologies* that would best implement them were designed and the ensuing learning *achievements* were identified. Somewhat later, the concept of *evaluation* was added whereby the achievement was compared to the original objectives in a feedback loop and allowed appropriate modifications to the original analysis to be set in train. Kerr (1967) wrote:

The Nuffield model for curriculum construction is becoming a standard pattern. Teams of school teachers, college lecturers and university consultants backed by advisory committees draft new programmes which are tried out in selected schools. As a result of feedback from the pupils and teachers, the courses are modified and put to more extensive trial before publication. A wide range of course material is produced, including guides for teachers, texts for pupils, reference books, laboratory notes and background readers; newly designed apparatus and equipment; films, charts and models; and test instruments designed to measure specific outcomes of the course. . . . If the objectives of a course have been identified and described in concise operational terms, it is logically a simple exercise to identify those aspects of a course which it is desirable to evaluate and then to choose an appropriate instrument or technique for each job. It is likely that information would be sought about the feasibility of the objectives; about the suitability of the content and the methods by which it is taught; about the pupils' needs and their achievements; and about the effectiveness of teacher preparation, before and during service.

Figure 3

In their simplest form the early models of curriculum development looked like Figure 3. Such early models may have suffered from the limitation that they were largely formulated for use in the science areas of the curriculum. In consequence their development had a 'scientific' orientation which led developers to identify characteristics such as 'measurable behavioural activities'. Such an *objectives model* was seen to be inappropriate for many of the more expressive areas of the curriculum; for these, *process* models came to be established that focused more sharply on the experience of learning rather than on its end results. Associated with process models came the concept of *illuminative evaluation* developed from anthropological models. Parlett and Hamilton (1972) write:

> Illuminative evaluation is introduced as belonging to a contrasting 'anthropological' research paradigm. Attempted measurement of 'educational products' is abandoned for intensive study of the programme as a whole; its rationale and evolution, its operations, achievements and difficulties. The innovation is not examined in isolation, but in the school context or 'learning milieu'. . . . Observation, interviews with participants (students, instructors, administrators and others), questionnaires, and analysis of documents and background information are all combined to help 'illuminate' problems, issues, and significant programme features.

The growth of curriculum development through objective and process models and the associated evaluation techniques since the late

1950s has been one of the great growth areas of the 'education industry'. The development of curriculum projects has now covered almost all areas of the curriculum of all schools for all age groups and has spread to universities, colleges and most other educational institutions. An army of curriculum developers has been recruited; increasingly sophisticated techniques have been developed and libraries of books have been written. New specialist institutions for the promotion of curriculum development have burgeoned on both sides of the Atlantic.

The Schools Council

In England and Wales the most notable institution for curriculum development quickly became the Schools Council. Originally conceived in 1960 by the then Minister of Education, the Curriculum Study Group was set up in 1962 consisting of members of Her Majesty's Inspectorate, administrators and a few outside experts. The establishment of such a potentially powerful instrument of control by central government led to predictable anxiety and hostility. Representations from the National Union of Teachers and the Association of Educational Committees led to the translation of the Curriculum Study Group into the Schools Council for the Curriculum and Examinations which came into being on 1 October 1964. Since 1 April 1970 the Council has received half its income in the form of direct grant from central government through the Department of Education and Science; the other half from the local education authorities, each contributing in proportion to the number of pupils in their maintained schools. By 1974 some £5 million had been spent in the development of curriculum and examinations for and in the schools of England and Wales.

But despite the dominance of the Schools Council the work of curriculum development has been undertaken in a wide variety of organizations. Not only has the Nuffield Foundation continued to support extensive curriculum development but also a range of internationally established bodies such as the Ford Foundation and the Gulbenkian Foundation have involved themselves in the action. Curriculum development has been undertaken in a range of research institutes, universities, colleges and schools, some setting up special units for the purpose such as the Goldsmiths' Curriculum Laboratory in the University of London. There can be few schools that have not played some part in curriculum development either as participants in a project or on their own initiative. Courses in curriculum development have become part of the routine socialization of initial and in-service teacher education. It is not the purpose of this volume to describe the complex paths of curriculum development; there are many detailed accounts, notably that by Stenhouse (1975), *An Introduction to Curriculum Research and Development.*

Power and the curriculum

Of central concern to sociologists are the implications of change for the distribution of power. The arrival of curriculum development not only institutionalized the process of curriculum change; it also helped to institutionalize the political struggle for power over the curriculum. And as Esland (1971) has noted, the very existence of curriculum change may also reflect a changing balance of power over the distribution of knowledge in society. But the most important development of the opportunities for political initiatives appeared to arise from the establishment of the major bodies for curriculum reform, notably the Schools Council. Control over such bodies offers the prospect of exercising major influence over curriculum that previously would have been inconceivable. The point was not lost on the professional associations representing both teachers and local authority administrators, who saw the prospect of a marked loss or gain of professional autonomy with predictable clarity. Indeed, as we have seen, it was the initial hostile reactions of the professional groups that led to the translation of the Curriculum Study Group into the Schools Council itself. Manzer (1970) noted that 'There was fear that the prestige of the Minister behind any recommendations of the group would make them practically mandatory'.

The formal structure of the Council shows that the teachers' union representatives together have a majority on all the main decision-making committees, ranging from the subject committees with their advisory powers through to the three steering committees with their capacity to recommend or reject projects and ultimately the programme committee which has the ultimate decision-making role. In the main council and also in the various examinations committees the situation is similar.

The search for teacher autonomy was not confined to the workings of the Schools Council at national level. Each project supported by the Council came to have an advisory committee in which teachers were represented, frequently forming a majority. Decisions on the schools in which project activity should take place are commonly made by local professional representatives acting either informally or constituted into a committee for the purpose. But it may be argued that it is at the level of schools rather than the Schools Council that the battle for professional power and autonomy in the new situation was most keenly fought. Certainly there are good reasons for expecting the implications of curriculum change to be responded to sensitively in the schools. Stenhouse writes: 'the school has a hierarchy of status and power. Curriculum and organisation change disturbs that allocation of status. Integration threatens the power base of subject departments. The introduction of new subjects increases the competition for resources and may create new opportunities for promoted posts' (1975, p. 171).

An editorial in *The Teacher* (1964), the official journal of the National Union of Teachers, wrote that the Schools Council was 'an organisation which can cock a snook at the Ministry any time it likes, yet has no powers of dictation over the man in the classroom'. Even when decisions have been made, projects completed and final reprints published, the Council has no mandatory power to put them into practice: the final decision remains with the school and the teachers. At best the Council can try to persuade through diffusion, aftercare and teachers' centre activities.

The reality of curriculum change

So far we have only outlined a political structure wherein changes in the balance of power in curriculum determination may take place. To what extent is such change actual rather than merely potential? Have teachers effectively won power over the definition, distribution and evaluation of knowledge in the curriculum with all that this implies for the process of social control? Has the dominance of the received perspective been replaced at least in part by the reflexive perspective espoused by many participants in curriculum development? Has the new situation led to an effective restructuring of the curriculum that embraces the new consciousness we have noted? In short, has the underlying nature rather than the surface content of the curriculum changed?

The picture is confused by the changes in structure and resource distribution that have unquestionably taken place. There is no doubt that schools have responded to the new curricula. It is not difficult to find substantial numbers of schools wherein Nuffield science, the Humanities Curriculum project, design education and many other project-supported innovations are taking place. Integrated studies departments, design departments and community service units are now common organizational characteristics of many secondary schools. Project publications sell in large numbers; one local education authority spent £1 million to enable teachers to use Nuffield science in its schools. The Schools Council Publishing Company has become a large and effective organization working in liaison with a very wide range of commercial publishers (Mothersole, 1975).

There is no doubt that projects influence the politics of the schools. Certainly at an individual teacher level personal political issues regularly arise in decisions whether or not to participate, at various levels of involvement, in curriculum development activities in their classrooms. Important professional consequences can arise from successful participation in a successful project, especially if it is one that is viewed favourably by professional colleagues within and outside the school.

Yet the educational system has in the past provided abundant evidence that changes in administrative structures, allocation of resources and location of personnel make no necessary change in the distribution of achievement of opportunity and power that is experienced either by the teachers themselves or by their students. Still less does it appear to make a necessary difference to the nature and determination of social control. To answer the questions of a previous paragraph, we shall have to look beneath the structural changes and examine the interaction processes that take place at a time of curriculum change.

An interaction map of curriculum development

In order to do this it will be useful to set out an interaction map of curriculum development. Whilst it is not possible in such a map to take account of the full range of exchanges that occur or to represent a full range of development strategies, it is suggested that some of the most commonly recurring interactions are as follows:

1   The preliminary *identification of the possibility of curriculum change* in, or beyond, existing defined areas of the curriculum. This may be done by teachers, heads, administrators or researchers. It may spring from many sources. Sometimes it may arise from the work of isolated teachers responding to problems of motivation or discipline in their classrooms. It may arise from a desire by enthusiasts to incorporate 'new' knowledge or previously unincorporated knowledge into the school curriculum, for example technological activities or sixth form psychology programmes. It may spring from response to external

pressure groups. At this stage there is likely to be little politicization of the discussion of the possibility of new curriculum within the school system.

2   The establishment of a *pressure group* within the system consisting of teachers and other personnel who have come to identify the changes as being not only desirable, but also feasible and in accord with an ideological perspective to which they subscribe. At this point the communication networks of the system — the educational press, conferences, the Inspectorate and advisers who pass between schools — may play an important part. By this stage a *de facto* commitment to a restructuring perspective will have been reached; there will also be at least an implied professional consensus about the desirability of the change promoted so that significant challenges from other teachers can rest either unsaid or at least discounted. Some informal work along the new lines will already have been begun in a number of schools as part of the establishment of a preparatory case.

3   Having established the area of proposed development and partially legitimated it, a further stage in legitimacy is then attempted in a search for *institutional support*. Often an established organization can be persuaded to lend its standing by offering to take on responsibility for a project if, and when, it is funded. Such an organization can be a university department or college, a local education authority or a professional subject organization. It may even be possible, given an adequate time-scale, to establish a new organization should no existing organization be available or suitable. The legitimacy added by an institution can take effect in many ways. The institution can enlist the services of its own or outside 'establishment' figures, call conferences, promote publicity and provide machinery in which negotiations with other institutions and associations may take place.

4   At this stage it is possible to proceed to draw up and submit to a funding body detailed proposals for a *development project* that set out a detailed case for the new curriculum and the advantages that it has over existing curriculum content and practice. The proposals will also demonstrate the support of a wide range of professional opinion. The appropriate documents will have been drawn up after exhaustive informal discussions with the staff of the proposed funding body. It is important that thought be given to the likely questions of the professional teacher representatives on the funding body. Issues such as the likelihood of placing additional burdens on school staffs; the possibility of conflict with existing established teaching interests; the provision

of opportunities for the classroom teacher to regulate his degree of involvement; all these are likely to be issues upon which assurance will be needed.

5   At this stage funds may be made available and *the execution of the project* is likely to be authorized though possibly in a modified form. The veracity of the previous stages will now be put to its most crucial test. Project staff will have to be appointed; they will need to satisfy tests not only of their subject competence but also of their professional acceptability. Negotiations to ensure an acceptable range of trial schools in which the project may be based will have to be conducted in liaison with local professional bodies and with the heads and teachers of the schools themselves. A mode of working that ensures the active participation and responsibility of the staff in the schools will almost certainly be a prerequisite of a continuing productive relationship between the project team and the classroom teachers. In these negotiations it is possible that the processes or objectives to which the project is directed may receive further substantial modification.

6   If the subject area falls within the secondary school curriculum it is likely that parallel *negotiations with the public examination boards* will be initiated that will in due course lead to the new subject content forming an acceptable basis for examination. Unless such arrangements can be effected, the new curriculum is likely to be relegated to the timetables of junior forms, minority time or else to students who are not considered to be eligible to take public examinations. Most project teams would argue that the area of the curriculum they are concerned with is important and has a valid claim to be included in any final assessment of students' school achievement. In consequence examinations based on the new curriculum should replace or augment those based upon previous or less important components of the curriculum. Whilst it is relatively easy to adapt examination arrangements to take account of the new curriculum development based upon behavioural objectives, it is more difficult to base examinations on new curricula adopting a process model. Though the public examining boards display an increasing flexibility of approach and are willing to accept course work and project assessment and even submissions by groups of candidates, this is still an area of considerable difficulty for many of the new curricula and can lead to conflict between the teacher representatives on the curricular project committee and their teacher colleagues on the committees of the examining boards.

7   Quite apart from the public examination system the project will

need to build into its organization some *evaluation arrangements*. These may be, depending on the nature of the project, either of a formal objective nature or of a less formal illuminative evaluation style that will throw light on the learning and experience and achievement of pupils. Not only is evaluation necessary to comply with the now orthodox rituals of curriculum development but it is also a tool that allows the further advocacy of the strategy of the project. It also offers a useful structural device for ensuring the participation of the classroom teachers in assessing the outcomes of the project.

8   Some method of *publishing* the findings of the project will almost certainly be called for by the funding body. Participation in the project, no matter how large, must inevitably be restricted to a relatively small number of schools and teachers. Some methods of making the results more widely available outside the project after its completion is called for. This will be further justified by the widespread support that the project will have had to display before funding. It will also be seen to be necessary in order to attempt to maximize the 'return' for the investment of funds into the development.

9   Closely associated with 8 will be the problem of *diffusion* whereby the project team will be expected, and usually feel the need, to provide some sort of follow-up so that the materials produced will be used with some guidance by teachers unfamiliar with them. Many strategies may be felt to be necessary at this stage to ensure that the ideas of the project take root and become part of the normal crop in a wide range of relevant schools.

It is clear that in the working-out of these stages the restructuring initiative of the original innovators has to respond to many adjustments in order to fit the needs of a wide range of institutions, organizations, schools, administrators, examining boards and the requirements of the funding body. When the project has finally taken place and the results have been made available to the system at large, how much remains? Are the adjustments in total so great as to translate a restructuring initiative into so pale a shadow of its original form that the received perspective remains in being, hardly dented by the lifespan of a curriculum development project?

We shall try to answer this question by focusing on the negotiations that take place at two levels, with the funding body and within the schools.

Negotiations within the Schools Council

For an account of events within the major British funding body, the Schools Council, we may first of all begin with the work of Manzer (1970). His view is essentially one of consensus in which the political culture is seen as a set of common values with the political structure operating within it to agreed limits; responding to demands for education by producing educational policies that allow the demands to be implemented within the agreed culture. The self-balancing system is operated by a largely autonomous educational sub-government, consisting of local and national educational administrators and teachers.

In the light of this system Manzer suggests that the Curriculum Study Group sprang from a central government initiative that was responding, exceptionally, to the demands arising outside the educational system. Faced with its existence, the educational sub-government adapted and the Schools Council was created. This new institution formed an arena in which the exercise of the educational sub-government, now taking heed of the new needs, was able to operate. This however was only feasible because the new organization had power only to make recommendations agreed by all its member interests. In consequence it presented no real threat to the existing equilibrium.

Some of the assumptions of Manzer's analysis will be already apparent, notably the assumption of consensus of a kind that is seldom evident in educational discussion, both within the school and in the wider society, and the further assumption that the demand for education and the appropriate response can be identified and assimilated within the existing consensus by the sub-government group. The Schools Council is seen as an instrument whereby new demands are being quickly assimilated by a relatively permanent elite which can formulate an agreed programme of curriculum innovation. Manzer's work is criticized by Young (1972), who writes: 'he manages to make problems unproblematic and thus fails to raise questions for research or the hypotheses that require data to support them that might generate new enquiries'.

An alternative view from that of Manzer is to see the Schools Council as a body that reinforces the existing definition, distribution and evaluation of knowledge, working substantially within the received perspective. Such a view would see the Council as making curricular recommendations within the traditionally accepted definitions of knowledge and ability and enforcing them by its indirect but effective control of 'new resources' and the authority that derives from the nature of its sponsorship and the size of its budget. A number of commentators see the Schools Council and curriculum development as a whole as authoritarian. Delamont (1976) writes of curriculum developers 'who shift the control of knowledge away from the teacher'.

There is certainly evidence to suggest that in parts of its work the Schools Council has tended to embrace traditional dichotomies of 'academic' and 'non-academic' children of a kind that are normally found within the received perspective. Certainly the major focus of much of the early development work of the Council was to anticipate the problems that secondary schools would experience after the raising of the school-leaving age when they would be faced with substantial numbers of children who were not committed to the examination programmes that had, up to that time, been the main or even the only offering of the schools for their older pupils. Using various descriptions of such children, ROSLA, Newsom, non-academic or average, the Council sponsored a number of projects that focused on the needs of these pupils and not on the more able, academic children. Such emphases may be juxtaposed against other projects, particularly the science programmes initiated by Nuffield which had a clear orientation towards the more able pupils that can be traced through from the early drafting stages that were undertaken within the largely independent school membership of the Science Masters Association. Not only in science but also in mathematics and geography, separate development projects have existed that seem to reflect an academic/non-academic division of curriculum.

It has also been widely claimed that the Schools Council has shown itself more ready to fund projects from the lower-status areas of the curriculum that cater predominantly for less able pupils in the schools. In such areas the outcomes of new curricula, however radical and restructured, would tend to be less likely to have significant consequences on the system of social control and the distribution of power in society. One of the most widely publicized events in the Council's history was its decision not to continue to sponsor the Humanities project proposal to develop curriculum materials to further the discussion of racial issues (the proposed 'Race Pack') — a proposal which had inescapable implications for social control in contemporary society. Certainly some of the most radical departures in the new curricula arising from Schools-Council-funded projects have been in apparently less significant areas, for example, in the Drama project (McGregor,

1976) and the Design and Craft Education project (Eggleston, 1976a). And even to talk of subjects is a reminder that a major part of the Schools Council's development work in curriculum and, incidentally, in examinations too, has been focused on the long-established subject divisions of the curriculum: a pattern in part imposed by the organizational structure of the Council where the subject committees form an essential first stage for almost all decisions on the funding of new projects.

There is, however, considerable evidence that many members of the secretariat and of the committees of the Schools Council are sharply aware of these criticisms and have sought to move to a more radical restructuring approach to the curriculum and examinations. On the curriculum side a notable attempt was in the establishment of its Working Party on the Whole Curriculum: a wide-ranging and unstructured attempt to look fundamentally at the *rationale* and development of the curriculum as a whole in a way that was neither possible for the members of individual projects nor readily accessible to the members of the established committees of the Council. The published report of the Working Party (Schools Council, 1975) displays a radical stance and comments perceptively on many of the underlying curricular positions adopted by the Council and its projects. Yet even in this committee the political necessity of the Council to ensure that it had a wide and representative membership, the administrative necessity to demonstrate that it had taken cognizance of a wide and balanced range of opinions and the practical necessity, despite the exploration of many radical alternatives, that its report should fit into the Council's series of working papers meant that its restructuring impetus, though remaining visible, became somewhat muted. Moreover, as a working party, its discussions were isolated from the main committee procedures of the Council; critics might suggest that creating a licensed enclosure for its more radical associates and giving them a time-consuming activity to perform within it effectively neutralized their potential influence on the main organization, which was allowed to run on without hindrance.

Young (1972), in his detailed critique of the Schools Council, takes a somewhat similar view of the role of the Council to that of the previous paragraphs. But he also suggests that, in addition to the academic emphases of the Council, there are also parallel emphases on good practice that also derives from an essentially received perspective. He cites in particular the Council's curriculum projects on the middle school and English in the middle years as examples. He also makes the interesting point that there is no existing evidence that suggests that the teachers' unions' representatives act in the pursuit of any coherent policy of professional autonomy; indeed they may be prevented from doing so because this in itself would limit the autonomy of their class-room teacher members. In consequence, he sees little challenge to the received perspective from the organized teachers' representatives' majorities on the Council's committees.

While the evidence for the identification of the prevailing orienta-tions of the Schools Council is incomplete and, as Young concedes, largely unobtainable, there is certainly little ground for arguing that the Schools Council, despite a number of localized achievements, has made a widespread breakthrough in restructuring the curriculum of the schools. Conversely, there is evidence that the Council and its projects have embodied and reinforced predominantly received positions; reflexive critics such as Young have little difficulty in drawing attention to this. But it is possibly a mistake to look for major restructuring initiatives in a macro organization such as the Schools Council. Such a search may better be focused at the other end of the curriculum process, the work taking place in the school and in its classrooms. It is to this area that we shall now turn.

Negotiations within the school and its classrooms

One of the pioneers in the examination of the incidence of curriculum development in the schools has been Hoyle (1969a and b). He sets out a profile for the 'innovative school':

> For any curriculum innovation to become an effective improvement on an existing practice it must 'take' with the school and become fully institutionalized. Genuine innovation does not occur unless teachers become personally committed to ensuring its success. Unless this commitment occurs, new methods and materials may eventually be permanently relegated to store-cupboards, or used only in an unsystematic manner.

An essential characteristic of the innovative school is that it does not suffer from 'tissue rejection' whereby an innovation does not 'take' with a school because the social system of the school is unable to absorb it into its normal functioning.

Hoyle's emphasis on the school as a key variable in the process of curriculum change came as a useful corrective to the early modes of curriculum development where initiatives were 'made available to schools' by carefully selected expert teams usually working at some distance from the classroom. Increasingly, curriculum developers have sought to establish a partnership with teachers and to develop project activities that are seen by teachers to relate to the conditions of their school, their students and their resources.

The nature of the changes that occur when curriculum development reaches the school and the classroom is of crucial importance. It is here, above all else, that we must ask whether it amounts to a fundamental restructuring of knowledge with the redistribution of power that it implies, or alternatively, is it just a process of surface readjustment that may do no more than reinforce the received perspectives and long-standing patterns of control? All inquiries confirm that the crucial determinants of the nature of whatever change does take place comes from the headteachers and the classroom teachers. In the primary schools studied by Taylor, Reid, Holley and Exon (1974), the influence of teachers far outweighed any influence exercised by parents, research organizations, local authorities and all other outside agencies.

A central figure in the affairs of the school is, predictably, the head. Hoyle (1972) has noted that his position springs almost inevitably from his traditional authority, his own view of the school, his contact with those who bring knowledge of innovation from other schools and the expectations that surround his role. Brown (1971), in a study of the implementation and initiation of change in primary schools, reported that in all cases the decision to innovate was made by the headteacher; it was he who became aware of the possibility, considered it, evaluated it and ultimately decided whether or not to adopt the innovation. It is equally clear that heads and class teachers see their institutional conditions of work as the paramount determinant in deciding whether or not to involve themselves in innovative curricula. The immediate problems of motivation, discipline and resources are uppermost in their minds. Shipman, Bolam and Jenkins (1974) showed in their investigation of the response to the Keele Integrated Studies project that teachers displayed very considerable interest in the immediate prospects that the project offered for their day-to-day work, but very little interest in either the underlying philosophy or the objectives of the project. Jenkins and Shipman (1976), commenting upon this finding, write:

Few heads or integrated studies teachers could remember precisely how they got involved. They remembered meetings and circulars.

But there do not seem to have been many discussions of pros and cons among staff resulting in a reasoned decision to join. Most schools seem to have drifted into the innovation. Indeed, in five of the thirty-eight schools the teachers insisted that they had never joined, despite receiving the normal quota of advice, visits and materials.

A particularly interesting feature of the work of Shipman, Bolam and Jenkins was the way in which decision making on curriculum change took place. In eight of the thirty-eight schools participating in the Keele project, teachers claimed that they had been given no choice in the matter by the head; in two others, teachers claimed that a new head had taken the school out of the project against their wishes. Yet heads were convinced that such decisions had been by agreement; in fact this seems to have been by informal and often brief discussion rather than by any extended and formal decision-making process. Brown (1971) in her study of primary schools asserts that 'in the majority of cases no staff meetings were held'. Yet however projects were introduced or abandoned, heads were universally confident in their judgment on curriculum development and almost without exception saw their decisions as being successful ones.

Another recurring characteristic of curriculum development is the decline of school commitment to a project. Enthusiasm for an innovation is likely to be greatest at the outset. The prospect of a new and 'free' supply of ideas and even resources for the work of the classroom are attractive, especially if the project promises to focus on some of the more difficult areas of the curriculum where the school is experiencing problems (perhaps this in itself goes some way to explain the tendency of the Schools Council to focus attention on work for 'less able' students). There is always the prospect that this project will be 'the project', participation in which will bring fame and renown to the school and its teachers. Certainly the project, when initially presented by enthusiastic advocates backed by the legitimation that they have built up in the formative stages, is likely to exercise at least some influence on the thinking of the staff.

But as time passes the situation is likely to change. There will inevitably be some problems, possibly many, in the use and adaptation of the project to the work of the school. Some successful existing curriculum practices may be challenged and even have to be abandoned if the project is to be taken fully. Timetable changes and other organizational disruption may be necessary. Key members of staff who are most heavily involved in the project may move to different appointments;

this happened frequently in some of the Keele project schools. In some cases the teacher's very involvement in the project is likely to be a factor in his upward professional mobility. The replacement members of staff may be less interested in the project and certainly will have lacked the initial impetus of the early stages in the school.

Faced with the inevitable difficulties, deprived of the initial leadership in the school and unwilling to abandon successful longstanding practices, marginal staff tend to become more marginal, even disaffected. At the end of the day the state of most projects seems to be one of fragmentation. Some teachers will retain a substantial commitment to some but not all of the ideas, methods and objectives of the project; most will have adopted bits and pieces and used them to modify, to a greater or lesser extent, their existing practices. Packages will have been taken apart; some of the contents adopted and others discarded. Project methods will have been interspersed with non-project methods. The result will be a *mélange* composed of items from various projects, a range of opinions on how it may be used, further material generated within the school from time to time, the whole gradually modifying the teacher's longstanding curriculum in a highly pragmatic and often unplanned way. For the teacher who is not involved in the trial schools and only learns about the projects when the final materials or reports are eventually published, the direct contribution made by the project to his day-to-day teaching is likely to be even less.

Shipman (1974) points out the issues clearly in his conclusion to an article entitled 'The Impact of a Curriculum Project':

The salient points are that the school which is likely to successfully introduce and implement a planned innovation would:
—have teachers who would feed back information to the project
—have teachers who would accumulate supplementary material
—have teachers who had volunteered knowing that they would be involved in a lot of work
—reorganize its timetable to provide planning time for teachers involved in innovation
—have a head teacher who supported the innovation but did not insist on being personally involved
—have a low staff turnover among key personnel
—be free of any immediate need to reorganize as part of a changing local school structure.

It could be argued however that if you could find such a school there would be no point in trying to get it to change.

Does curriculum development bring about change?

In the light of our discussion, can we talk in any meaningful way of a restructuring perspective? Is the whole impact of curriculum development on the schools spasmodic and largely inconsequential? Can effective restructuring take place when teachers are for the most part uninterested in planning and curriculum objectives and even the heads who have taken modest restructuring initiatives are, for the most part, not even seen to be doing so by their staff?

To find an answer we must move away from the illusory models of rational development and study the realities of school life. In their study of the Keele project, Shipman, Bolam and Jenkins (1974) noted the contagious effects of one feature of the project. They noticed that in many of the schools the project activities were, for the most part, confined to juniors or non-examination students. The older examination candidates were, however, very alert to the news of the project taking place in other classes and expressed their enthusiasm to take part in the investigation of the apparently interesting and relevant contemporary problems themselves. The support of students, particularly that of the elite group of able pupils in the schools, reinforced the underlying orientations of the project powerfully and in several cases led to its extension to the programmes of the more able pupils.

The contagion effect was also to be seen in the Schools Council/ Nuffield Foundation Humanities project with its strong emphases on the teacher's role as an impartial chairman rather than as a person with a committed point of view. Macdonald (1973) notes that the introduction of this mode of teaching by teachers within the project was seen by students in the schools as offering an attractive non-authoritarian alternative style of teaching. Once this style was seen to be established within a school there was considerable pressure on the remainder of teachers to adopt it, particularly in subject areas that tended to overlap with the topics of the Humanities project.

In the new curriculum in design education (Eggleston, 1976a) a similar situation arises. Teachers committed to curricular approaches with a heavy emphasis on craft skill learning as an end in itself found themselves working with teachers who were adopting new problem-oriented approaches involving a wide range of craft skills that were used as a means rather than an end. The process of adjustment, where the 'skill' teachers came to participate in the new approaches and adapted their enthusiasm for craft skills to a new context that was not only more acceptable to the students but also more successful in satisfying their original purposes, has all the elements of a genuine restructuring process in that it allowed teachers and students far greater access to power in a design and construction context than hitherto. Certainly the curriculum changes that sprang from these personal readjustments were far more fundamental than those which sprang solely from the administrative reorganization wherein a design department was set up as an organizational feature of the school.

It is important, however, to recognize that, though effective restructuring of the curriculum requires more fundamental adjustments than those of organizational change alone, it may none the less be sparked off and reinforced by organizational change. A good example of the link between organizational change and restructuring may be seen in the sixth form. For many years this has been the centrepiece of the British system of state secondary education. Essentially it has consisted of those students who are voluntarily remaining at school after minimum leaving age and who are committed to continuing academic study. Not surprisingly it has been characterized by a strong commitment to the received perspective. There are particularly close links between sixth form teachers and the universities and the examination boards, as Taylor, Reid and Holley (1974) confirm. Yet with the onset of comprehensive secondary school reorganization in Britain, major organizational changes arise that challenge the longstanding arrangements. As Neave (1975) has shown, increasing numbers of students in the comprehensive schools enter the sixth form to take non-academic and non-examination programmes. Moreover, the structure of open choice in many comprehensive schools means that an increasing number of students make a decision to undertake academic study at a later stage than formerly, entering the sixth form to read, initially, for qualifications that would normally have been taken before admission to the sixth form. In consequence, new curricula become necessary to match the changed academic and social situation. A good example is the new curriculum in integrated science for the sixth form sponsored by the Nuffield Foundation. The very concept of integrated as opposed to specialist science in the sixth form would have been unacceptable in many schools in the recent past. The new curricula have obvious utility. They allow the study of science in the sixth form by those students who have followed a diverse range of previous science activity, possibly in various integrated forms, in their earlier years of schooling. They also hold open the prospect of specialist scientific study subsequently in the sixth form that is compatible with the extended time-scale of sixth form education that Neave has noticed. The ensuing legitimation and acceptance of integrated study, especially in such a prestigious area as the natural sciences now occupy, has a profound influence on the remainder of the sixth form curriculum in the new comprehensive schools that is amounting to a fundamental restructuring of the definition, distribution and evaluation of knowledge.

The restructuring process also receives reinforcement outside the schools by other organizational changes. Chief amongst these are the examinations boards which, as we have suggested, are showing themselves increasingly ready to respond to new curricula and integrated approaches in general. Integrated science may now be offered as an examination subject not only at O level but also at the pre-university A level examinations. Not only the knowledge content of the examination requirements but also the response to them may be in a form that relates to a newly developed project methodology. Increasingly, examinations are based upon some aspect of project or course work either in place of, or as well as, conventional written papers. This usually takes the form of a recognition of the kind of inquiry-based or problem-solving work that many of the new curriculum developments have adopted as their methodology. In many projects the most important stage is now seen to lie not so much in the achievement of funding or even the acceptance of the project into our schools but rather in the recognition of the examination boards that the new approaches can be recognized as 'examinable', as an acceptable component in the student's measured school achievement. Thus, a critical stage in the Design and Craft Education project was the early recognition by one of the CSE examination boards that students in the trial schools could take a special CSE examination, 'A Course of Studies in Design', that reflected the project's approaches and was based predominantly on a detailed record of problem-solving activities in a design project. Similar examinations are now regularly available in a number of CSE boards; A level GCE examinations in design are also available.

The redistribution of knowledge

We have now reached a point in our consideration of curriculum development where we may see important links with the issues raised in previous chapters. The indirect but effective consequences that appear to spring from the interplay of staff and student roles, structural reorganization and the new curricula can be seen to have major restructuring potential. Hoyle (1972) suggests that changes in the deep structure of the school are matched by changes in the deep structure of knowledge. Certainly the relevance of Bernstein's curriculum codes becomes apparent and the importance of the moves towards integrated codes becomes clear (it is interesting in this connection to note that, in post-secondary education, there is evidence of a parallel move towards integrated codes in the universities, polytechnics and the advanced colleges of further education; see Eggleston, 1975). There are also parallel curricular initiatives such as, for instance, the Nuffield Foundation Physics Interface project on the first year physical sciences curriculum of university students.

There are still many uncertainties in the process of curricular change. Though we have identified the changes in definition, distribution and evaluation of knowledge it is still difficult to identify how fully the consequences of such change have taken place. How widespread is the redistribution of knowledge in practice? Is it that the newly defined and evaluated knowledge is still being made available to the same group of students who received the formal versions? Almost certainly the answer is 'yes' to a large extent. But the annual statistics of the DES in the past decade suggest that overall an increasing proportion of all school leavers enter and achieve success in the various public examinations. The annual statistics of universities and polytechnics for a similar period suggest that an increasing percentage of the age group seeks to enter some form of tertiary education; one of the reasons for the widespread concern about financial restrictions in tertiary education in Britain in the mid-1970s springs from this knowledge and the belief that further development is likely to be necessary in order to meet the increasing demand. This demand is foreseen as continuing, notwithstanding the sharp absolute decline in birth-rate figures that will become increasingly apparent in total numbers in schools and tertiary education in the 1980s. And Neave (1975) suggests that in schools he has examined there is evidence that indicates that there are some redistributions in the educational and social background of students reaching the sixth form and continuing into tertiary education and beyond. In particular, Neave identified a number of students who were successfully participating in the work of the sixth form despite their previous failure in the examination for admission to the academic grammar schools held at the age of 11. And by implication a number of the students who would, under a previous regime, have been participating in the sixth form had either failed to reach it or to succeed within it.

Perhaps inevitably the evidence for restructuring is obscure. Are there any ways in which we can move towards greater clarification of the issues? Can we, in particular, help the teacher to avoid the fate that Owen (1973) ascribes to him of 'taking part in a conflict he does not fully understand'? So far we have identified the conditions of curriculum change and in particular the critical roles of heads, teachers and students in bringing about a restructuring of the situation, however unplanned or spasmodic the actual curriculum change in the school may be. Yet even on this evidence there is enough to identify the process as one of restructuring; the examples quoted the Keele Integrated Studies project, the Humanities project, the changes in design education and in the sixth form; all four indicate some shifts of power between teachers and teachers, between students and students and between teachers and students.

Can restructuring take a more coherent and more positive form? Are there strategies that can allow us to approach the heart of the matter more directly? To answer these questions we shall have to face more squarely the essentially political nature of the school curriculum and the consequences that may spring from a sharper perception of the issues involved. We shall devote ourselves to this task in the concluding chapter.

Summary

We have considered curriculum development in the light of the ideological debates and the interplay of teacher and student roles explored in previous chapters. The process of curriculum development has been examined and the implications for the definition, distribution and evaluation of knowledge and social control explored at the macro level (the Schools Council) and the micro level (the school). It has been suggested that though the evidence of restructuring at the macro level is slight, there is clear though indirect evidence of a restructuring process taking place at the micro level.

The politics of curriculum knowledge

Above and around the practice of curriculum there is a great deal of political 'noise' and distraction which has formed a continuing background to the discussion of the previous chapters. We have heard clarion calls such as 'the inalienable right of teachers to teach what they like'. We have also heard teachers deploring the tyranny of the authority of the examination boards, the 'project' and the textbook. We have teachers and students caught between the cross-fire of the politics of educational administrators, curriculum development organizations and professional organizations.

In writing of the politics of the curriculum there is an even greater risk of falling into the temptation of mistaking superficial noises for fundamental issues. Before we immerse ourselves in the final task of this volume and draw the components of the previous chapters together within a political action framework it will be useful, in order to avoid distraction, to take stock of the argument so far.[1]

The analysis so far

The volume commenced with a preliminary justification for the sociological analysis of the curriculum, drawing attention to the central importance of the definition, distribution and evaluation of knowledge in societies; a central political theme that has recurred throughout the volume. Faced with the ensuing task of identifying the complexities of curriculum practice, we adopted, with some qualification, a systems approach in order to provide a *description* (but not an analysis) of the situation in the schools.

Our analysis proper began with an historical exploration in which the long-running political conflict over the nature of knowledge and its implications for the distribution of power and social control could be clearly seen in the gradual development of the school curriculum. The conflict analysis was explored still further in the consideration of the contemporary ideological perspectives that underly the curriculum wherein the received perspective, with its strongly normative connotations, was juxtaposed against the reflexive perspective with its interpretative paradigm. We went on to identify the emergence of a restructuring perspective containing elements of both received and reflexive perspectives. The restructuring perspective promised to be not only a more useful tool for analysing curriculum but also one of greater sensitivity to the consciousness of the participants than the received perspective and of greater alertness to the structural realities of organizations than the reflexive perspective.

The three perspectives were then used to consider life in schools and classrooms. There appeared to be little doubt that the politics of curriculum played an important part in the roles of both teachers and students. But while the politics of the curriculum may operate at a latent level in the classroom there is no mistaking their manifest appearance in curriculum development where the real issues of power are played out publicly.

The continuing conflict

Unquestionably the political debate about curriculum is now a permanent, institutionalized feature of Western educational systems. In Britain one of the most uncompromising expositions of the received perspectives has been *Black Paper No. 4* (Cox and Dyson, 1974). Not only was this document virtually sold out before the day of publication, it subsequently became the best-selling new educational book of the year. The continuing strength of the received perspective may also be detected by the success with which members of the Campaign for Educational Standards address meetings throughout the country, drawing enthusiastic responses from their audiences.

Conversely there is equally little doubt that the reflexive perspective is deeply established in the minds of many thousands of teachers. Students in initial and in-service courses respond enthusiastically to advocates of reflexive approaches such as Labov and other writers in the field of applied socio-linguistics who have explored the logic of 'nonstandard' English (Stubbs, 1976). Labov (1969), in his work with New York ghetto children defined as linguistic failures by the schools, found that, by communicating with them in their non-standard language, he was able to identify substantial capacities for creative thinking, expression and general verbal performance. His work contains an important challenge to the received perspective emphasis on correct standard English usage as a basis for creative and expressive writing.

Yet another reflexive study that has become one of the most widely known in teacher training is that of Wax and Wax (1964), who showed how new curricula for North American Indian children in the reservation schools place a high valuation on 'white' knowledge and a lower valuation on 'Indian' knowledge. The cautionary tale of 'the Water project', in which the Indian children were defined as disadvantaged because of their unfamiliarity with plumbing and central heating systems, has become one of the standard references of a generation of teachers, heavily reinforced by its intensive use in the education programmes of the British Open University.

Conflicting solutions

But how may the reflexive consciousness respond to the plight of the 'non-standard English users' and the 'North American Indians' who are to be found in every school? How may they obtain a more favourable curriculum experience that not only allows them to be successful in the school but also to achieve status, recognition and the opportunity to experience and exercise power that is denied them by the regular curriculum?

The solution within the received perspective is usually seen as 'giving them a chance' to succeed in the regular curriculum; even providing a specially favourable distribution of resources that allow them to be taught in smaller classes, receive more intensive counselling and support and even be taught by better-paid teachers specially trained to assist them. Their difference becomes defined as an incapacity to perform well in the regular curriculum; an incapacity that later becomes labelled 'deprived' or 'handicapped'. With such a definition the solution is simple. If they can be brought to perform well in the regular curriculum then they cease to be either different or deprived but rather successful and adjusted.

The solution within the reflexive curriculum is to provide a range of acceptable alternative curricula which may be offered not only in the state schools but also in the free schools or 'schools without walls' set up to provide an even more radical range of alternatives than that normally found within the state system. The concept of the alternative curricula involves parity of esteem between different curricular per-formances. Non-standard English presentations may be equally esteemed with the standard English presentations. An 'Indian' water project can rate equally with a 'white' water project.

Both solutions present major difficulties. Both are likely to run counter to the administrative and cultural patterns of the school. We have already seen the problems faced by 'Miss Sanders' as she jumped from one type of solution to another, always finding new and unsuspec-ted hazards. But even if the solutions are applied by a resolute and far-seeing teacher, they are still likely to fall short of what is desired.

The received solution at best can work for limited numbers of chil-dren. The difficulty of this adjustment and the scarcity of school resources alone are probably enough to ensure this. But the politics of the received perspective with its emphasis on differentiation in the social structure mean that the number of people who can succeed and exercise power is always seen to be limited. Hargreaves (1967) showed in Lumley School that the restriction of opportunities to succeed was built into the structure of the school, reflecting the social system it served. The restraints on access to power appear to override and even determine the restraints on curriculum achievement.

Conversely the reflexive solution appears to be available for unlimi-ted numbers. It can make the immediate experience of curriculum more satisfying for many children. Yet it is arguable if the solution in itself will begin to make any change in the child's ability to contract-in to decision making in society; to free himself from the position at the receiving end and to move on to experience and exercise power. More probably, as White (1968) has reminded us, it will tie him more success-fully to his non-standard English ghetto or to his reservation, by reinforcing his identity therein and denying him an identity that has currency outside it.

Essentially both solutions are incomplete because both leave the existing structure of society intact. Halsey (1972), in his report on the British Educational Priority Areas project, makes it clear that education cannot tackle disadvantage and inequality alone; it must be part of a wider strategy of social restructuring. Jencks (1972) and many other writers have emphasized the limited potency of education as a tool of social engineering unaided. Tyler has drawn these arguments together in a valuable review of this field of literature (1977). Here we return to the basic political premiss with which the restructuring perspective was introduced in Chapter 4. How may the curriculum not only assist a wider range of students to enhance their expectation of power and the capacity to exercise it but also play its part in bringing about a social situation in which these expectations and capacities may be put to use. What action does the restructuring perspective lead us to?

There is no shortage of writers alerting us to the need to take action. Bourdieu (1973) suggests that educational processes exist to maintain only an illusion of participation, open competition, equality and democracy. He writes:

> This is only one of the mechanisms by which the academic market succeeds in imposing upon those very persons who are its victims, recognition of the existence of its sanctions by concealing from them the objective truth of the mechanisms and social motives that determine them.

Althusser distinguishes between what he calls *repressive* and *ideological* modes of social control (1971). He contrasts the relationship between the two modes, suggesting that the former works through external constraints such as the police and the military whilst the latter works through ideology (church, schools, communication media). Althusser regards educational systems as the most effective ideological devices in technological society. Not only do they ensure the necessary supply of skilled competence, they also institutionalize innovation in order to create new processes of production. In other words the mechanism of the school reproduces not only the skills needed as a precondition for production but also reproduces and socializes pupils into the necessary processes and attitudes which lead to a respect for the discipline necessary for production. Appropriate ideologies are seen to be reflected both within the character and type of educational institutions and through the curricula therein.

But the question still remains — how to undertake restructuring with the curriculum as a starting point. It is insufficient for Althusser to apologize patronizingly to '. . . those teachers who, in dreadful conditions, attempt to turn the few weapons they can find . . . against the ideology . . . in which they are trapped' (1971). The traps which teachers and pupils face in the course of their work must be seen as 'problems' to be explained, rather than merely taken as indicative of wider crises in society. It may well be that for Althusser and Bourdieu, problems such as deficient motivation, underachievement, truancy and 'deprivation' are examples of wider and deeper 'structural' contradictions. But for teachers and pupils these conditions provide the platform on which they work in continued conflict while they search for solutions.

The practice of restructuring

Let us now move on from the political theory of restructuring and look at political practices in the classroom. We have already noticed how restructuring can take place by contagion in the Humanities Curriculum project, the Integrated Studies project, in design education and elsewhere in the school curriculum. But how can these changes in the definition, distribution and evaluation of knowledge and the ensuing changes in access to power be made more regularly available so that their incidence does not depend so largely on chance?

An important precedent can be seen in the work of the Youth Service, the British system of informal leisure education for young people aged 14 to 18 that is conducted in close liaison with the schools. The Service comprises a wide range of statutory and voluntary organizations and is staffed by adult leaders, many of whom are also teachers or who have been trained as teachers. The developments in the Youth Service display a classic example of the demand for restructuring. Many of the members are those who have been defined by the schools as being destined for low-status adult roles; committed to 'the receiving end' by the selective procedures of the school. A recently completed study (Eggleston, 1976b) shows that, notwithstanding the experience of schooling, many members of the Youth Service still have a keen desire to 'count for something', as they put it, and turn to the Youth Service in the hope of finding opportunities to do so.

The Youth Service on the whole has not satisfied them. Traditionally it has only offered opportunities to participate in power and responsibility to a very limited number of members, usually those who comply most fully with the value systems of the various statutory and voluntary organizations that constitute the Service. For most members their inferior prospects are further reified by the experience of the Service. Yet in the past decade a number of experimental projects have occurred in which members have had the chance to participate responsibly and to take decisions in meaningful community contexts. Although these projects have arisen on the margins of the Youth Service they have achieved a substantial response, often considerably in excess of that enjoyed by the mainstream organizations. Essentially the projects have been in the field of welfare and have allowed young people to make valued contributions both to adults and to other young people in some kind of need – economic, emotional and social. Many of the activities have been undertaken in conjunction with adult organizations which have allowed the young people to participate on equal terms. These have included Shelter, Release, Child Poverty Action and a number of local agencies. Two elements of restructuring have occurred simultaneously. The young people have escaped from a 'youth organization' parameter; they have also been able to enter and participate in the power structure of significant adult organizations. Both changes have sprung from the new curriculum of the experimental wing of the Youth Service.

The new approaches present problems for the adult worker in the Youth Service that are parallel to those of the teacher involved in the similar changes in the school curriculum. His role is fundamentally different from the 'leadership' position characteristic of the Service and the schools. He is in a new situation of partnership with his members in activities in which his expertise may be no more and can even be less than theirs. Moreover, if he is to help his members to achieve an effective decision-making role in the community he will find himself involved with them in action that is essentially political in nature. Indeed he must act as their political advocate. But if he is to do this he is likely to find himself 'confronting' the existing power structure of which he himself is part. If the worker is not to lose faith – and face – with his members he requires a measure of integrity, political awareness and maturity that may be considerably in excess of that required in more 'traditional' situations.

There are also problems of aims. Both adults and members see the Youth Service as an opportunity to achieve adult role and status. Yet the similarity is dangerously misleading, for the providers commonly see adult status as being defined in their terms, whereas the members seek, in most cases, a chance to define their own. To respond to the clients calls for subtle yet fundamental differences in organization and adult-participation. The change required seems to be no less than a change to relationships of 'contract' rather than 'commitment', with all the implications for power and control that this raises.

Yet there are clear signs that the Youth Service as a whole is responding to the new approaches; increasingly the programmes of even the mainstream organizations are turning to approaches of this kind. Growing numbers of members find the curriculum of the Youth Service to be one in which they can prepare themselves to exercise power in a community context; to develop the skills whereby they can find the opportunities, present a political argument, develop a necessary degree of fluency and confidence and, perhaps of greatest importance, develop a capacity to engage in discussion with the housing managers, welfare officers, civil servants and the whole army of 'experts' who exercise effective control over the conditions of life of the majority of members of contemporary societies.

Many youth organizations have demonstrated convincingly that opportunities of this kind not only exist but can be successfully used by 'ordinary' young people. A notable recent case arose when a London high-rise housing block was partially destroyed by a gas explosion. The residents of Ronan Point, who had been 'housed' by the local housing authority found themselves with a new voice and a new capacity to communicate with the housing authority and its officers and architects. The discussions, in which young and old participated, are widely seen by architects and others concerned with public housing to have begun a new wave of communication between clients and experts which has had important consequences for the design of housing schemes.

The exercise of power

In exploring the concept of participatory democracy emerging within the Youth Service we have an interesting example of the twin process of curriculum change and curriculum-induced social change. Yet it is important to notice that one of the major findings of the Youth Service study was that young people were emphatic that they did not wish to change society fundamentally. Essentially they wished to 'count for something' in the kind of social system that they knew well. For some even the knowledge that the opportunity to do this was available was sufficient; they did not necessarily wish to practise it. A major problem of some of the adults in the early experimental projects was that they were too radical in their political and social views and thereby cut off from many of the members. Smith (1976) has suggested that students may be far more realistic than teachers in their demands for curricular codes in which realistic and recognizable contest may occur rather than integrated codes where the opportunities may be masked.

Do these findings indicate that once again we have achieved no more than a symbolic restructuring? In the view of many participants in the field this is not so. They point to the widespread opportunities for the experience of power that are available to young people and adults in contemporary social systems. For many this exists within the organized workers' unions which unquestionably exercise substantial economic and social power in most developed industrial societies. A similar situation obtains in local government where, as with the unions, there is often a dearth of candidates for office. With appropriate curricula of the kind already outlined, the opportunities for a wider spread of power may be more readily available, even within an existing social system. Certainly the Youth Service is able to point to a number of former members of the Service who are now exercising substantial power as union officers, local councillors and officers of a wide variety of local pressure groups and interest associations.

A close parallel to the work of the Youth Service is the Social Education project (Schools Council, 1974) which also provides an interesting alternative to conventionally oriented civics, social studies or 'community service' programmes, by suggesting that social education is as much concerned with developing skills for challenging, controlling and changing the environment as it is with creating social awareness. The emphasis is upon teachers and pupils critically researching social issues together, both within and out of school, in the attempt, not only to understand the politico-social forces which influence their lives, but also tentatively to construct strategies and philosophies to change those forces. 'Basically social education of this type is dependent upon a relationship between pupil and teacher which is democratic. They are colleagues, jointly seeking answers to questions about the problems and challenges of the immediate school and community. Responsibility for control in the classroom is shifted gradually from being principally that of the teacher to a joint responsibility of teacher and children' (Williams and Rennie, 1972). These writers also point out that collaborative action research in the community alone will not change political inequality, unless it is perceived within the wider context of cultural action and critique. They write: '. . . self help: identification of problems, initiation of action, must come from *within* the community and not be imposed from *outside*: it must come from "us" not "them" '.

Such an approach contrasts sharply with the received perspective approaches to social studies teaching which have focused mainly upon combating teacher and pupil ethnocentrism by examining social phenomena through the objective 'findings' and 'evidence' provided by positivistic social science. Students experience social science 'facts' as a solution to moral ambiguity, rather than as providing the grounds for scepticism and research into the procedures used in acquiring those facts. An unintended consequence of many social studies courses has been that pupils are channelled into understanding the social scientists' definitions of the world to the neglect of constructing 'data' and materials which reflect their own perceptions and comprehension of social phenomena and which will help them to participate effectively within them.

An essential feature of these restructuring approaches is to make *problematic* the nature of institutional relationships, cultural reproduction and transmissions and the whole apparatus of curriculum determination and practice. Not only those working within a received perspective but also those working in a restructuring perspective are required to reflect critically upon their aims, motives and assumptions. If, for example, problem-solving education is to be seen as something other than just a cognitive activity or an alternative means of solving the puzzles of school-based knowledge, then it is necessary to ask, in what sense does it awaken students and teachers to a shared understanding of the human condition? To what extent does it question existing knowledge and suggest alternatives? What is knowing for? A central argument of this volume is that curriculum is *best* practised by those who can answer such questions; that curriculum change can *only* be practised by those who can answer such questions. It is further argued that those who hold the received or the reflexive perspective have at best only incomplete knowledge; that the restructuring perspective presented in this volume offers the prospect of a fuller understanding that is always desirable and at times essential for those who participate in the school curriculum.

As developed in this volume the restructuring perspective on the curriculum is neither an instrument of social revolution nor oppression, as writers such as Bowles and Gintis (1976) suggest; neither is it a device for extreme relativism nor absolutism. Instead it is a model of curriculum appropriate for an actively democratic society consciously concerned not only about its educational arrangements but also about its total pattern of social institutions and the lives of its individual members. It is a model that constitutes the most likely outcome of the public debates on curriculum currently taking place in Western society and one that is almost certain to be reinforced by the many new initiatives in curriculum assessment and evaluation that are now being undertaken.

Notes

2 Sociological approaches to the school curriculum

1 The role behaviours of teachers and of students and their reinforcement by behavioural norms will be discussed fully in subsequent chapters.

2 Much consideration has taken place in schools, particularly in recent years, of the development of curriculum strategies so that statements of this kind may be made more explicit behavioural objectives and lead to the development of more 'effective' curricula. These issues will be discussed in the chapter on curriculum change in this book. An early example of the discussion of such strategies is by Taylor (1949).

3 None of this of course is to say that the unofficial, informal or hidden curriculum, any more than informal out-of-school education, lack organization and structure — indeed, in some ways they may be even more highly structured, as studies of the playground, the gang and the peer group have indicated.

3 The historical determination of the school curriculum

1 I am particularly grateful for the helpful comments of my colleague Dr M. A. Cruickshank on an early version of this chapter.

2 A useful critical review of the literature of the grammar school and university curriculum of the period 1500—1660 is that of Webster (1975).

3 The arguments for the curriculum in Latin are usefully explored by Campbell (1968).

4 Though as Hurt (1970) and other writers have noted, there is considerable evidence of longstanding irregular achievement entry.

5 The codification of the examination system with the introduction of the School Certificate Examinations in 1917 and the consequences for the curriculum have been examined by Banks (1955), ch. 7.

6 The development of examinations has, predictably, drawn professional attention to their control features and major attempts have been mounted to achieve teacher control of the examination system

and hence greater control of the curriculum. This issue is discussed more fully in subsequent chapters that deal with curriculum innovation and curriculum decision making.

7 The debate between the classical and scientific curricula persisted. R. W. Livingstone (1916), in his *A Defence of Classical Education*, asserted that the growth of science would lead to an attack on the classical education given to most public schools. H. G. Wells (1917) attacked Livingstone for 'a narrow, aristocratic conception of education unsuited to a democracy and cut off from the market place'.

8 Yet the net effect of the Crowther Report was to introduce a range of new flexibility into the sixth form curriculum, including new subjects and 'major' and 'minor' options.

9 It was this new realization of the role of the school that added a new importance to the longstanding conflict between church and state over the control of the schools. (This issue is fully discussed by Cruickshank, 1963.)

10 Though Lowndes also draws attention to the attempts of the elementary sector to establish its own identity through the trade, junior technical and secondary modern schools with a distinctive 'non-academic' curriculum that in no way sought to follow the high-status liberal classical curriculum of the grammar schools.

11 It may be that a contributory factor is the willingness of the more effective advocates of re-evaluation to shift to other professional roles achieving personally enhanced high status, notwithstanding their failure to achieve their original goals.

12 Williams (1961) suggests that there are two further types of curricula that can be seen in such resistant approaches. These are the democratically oriented curricula of the radical reformers espousing 'education for all' and the populist curricula of the working-class movement oriented to achieve relevance and participation. Yet as with Williams's two forms of high status education, the distinction is one between use and purpose rather than with content.

13 Curricular innovation was not, of course, unknown in church schools; Churchmen were sometimes highly innovative such as, for example, Richard Dawes in the village school at Kings Somborne, Hampshire in the 1840s.

4   Contemporary ideological perspectives on the curriculum

1 I am particularly grateful for the helpful comments of my colleague, Mr G. W. Powell, on an early version of this chapter.

2 This point has been reaffirmed in an interesting analysis by Apple (1975).

3 Even writers such as Illich and Reimer may, however, be accused of holding a given position. Holly (1973) writes: 'For libertarians they seem curiously addicted to authority centres, the criteria for which cannot be questioned or discussed — authors, museum-keepers, networks of "masters", "professional advisers" and "skill instruc-

tors". For a schooled imagination they would seem to substitute a
de-schooled credulity.'

4 It is interesting to note that curriculum theorists have been far more
concerned with Phenix's concept of knowing than with his concept
of knowledge; possibly because they feel, however subjectively, that
this surrounds him with a less ultimate form of restrictiveness.

5 An account of the historical development of these approaches is to
be found in Eggleston (1974).

5   Curriculum organization in the school — the teachers' role

1 There is an increasing literature of classroom observation that adds
corroboration to this view of the teacher's role as an agent of social
control. For a guide and critical commentary on this literature, see
Robinson's 'An Ethnography of Classrooms' (1974).

2 No attempt is being made here to suggest that these variables would
form part of any general attitude scales: they are chosen *ad hoc* as
the most suitable formulation for the study. However, once this
reservation has been made, it is fair to point out that the first two
pairs have much in common with Eysenck's conservative-radical
continuum and Oliver's idealist-naturalist continuum respectively.
Furthermore, the third pair is closely akin to Parsons's universalistic-
particularistic dichotomy, though much narrower since it is intended to apply specifically only to the particular situation under scrutiny. The last pair, in some ways derivative from the other three, is
listed separately here as likely to be fruitful in the analysis of specifically curriculum orientations.

8   The politics of curriculum knowledge

1 Some of the issues raised in this chapter are also discussed in Eggleston and Gleeson (1977).

Bibliography

Adamson, J. W. (1964), *English Education 1789–1902*, Cambridge University Press.

Althusser, L. (1971), 'Ideology and Ideological State Apparatuses: Notes towards an Investigation' in *Lenin and Philosophy and other Essays*, London, New Left Books.

Apple, M. W. (1975), 'Common-Sense Categories and Curriculum Thought' in J. B. MacDonald *et al., Schools in Search of Meaning*, Washington, Association for Supervision and Curriculum Development.

Baines, E. (1846), *Letters to Lord John Russell*, London, Simpkin Marshall.

Banks, O. (1955), *Parity and Prestige in English Education*, London, Routledge & Kegan Paul.

Bantock, G. H. (1968), *Culture, Industrialisation and Education*, London, Routledge & Kegan Paul.

Bantock, G. H. (1971), 'Towards a Theory of Popular Education' in R. Hooper (ed.), *The Curriculum Context, Design and Development*, Edinburgh, Oliver & Boyd.

Baratz, S. S. and Baratz, J. G. (1970), 'Early Childhood Intervention: the Social Science Basis of Institutionalised Racism', *Harvard Educational Review*, 40, 2, February.

Baron, G. and Howell, D. A. (1974), *The Government and Management of Schools*, London, Athlone Press.

Baron, G. and Tropp, A. (1961), 'Teachers in England and America' in A. H. Halsey, J. Floud and C. A. Anderson (eds), *Education, Economy and Society*, New York, Free Press.

Becker, H. (1963), *Outsiders: Studies in the Sociology of Deviance*, New York, Free Press.

Bell, G. (ed.) (1975), *The Schools Council*, London, Ward Lock.

Bell, R. and Prescott, W. (1975), *The Schools Council: A Second Look*, London, Ward Lock.

Beloe Report (1960), Ministry of Education, *Secondary School Examinations other than the GCE*, London, HMSO.

Berger, P. L. and Berger, B. (1972), *Sociology, a Biographical Approach*, New York, Basic Books, p. 295.

Berger, P. L. and Luckmann, T. (1971), *The Social Construction of Reality: a Treatise in the Sociology of Knowledge*, Harmondsworth, Penguin.

Bernbaum, G. (1974), 'Countesthorpe College' in Centre for Educational Research and Innovation, *Case Studies of Educational Innovation: III. At the School Level*, Paris, OECD.

Bernstein, B. B. (1970), 'Education cannot Compensate for Society', *New Society*, 26 February.

Bernstein, B. B. (1971), 'On the Classification and Framing of Educational Knowledge', in M. F. D. Young (ed.), *Knowledge and Control*, London, Collier-Macmillan.

Bernstein, B. B. (1975), 'Changes in the Coding of Educational Transmissions on the Curriculum' in *Class, Codes and Control*, Vol. 3, London, Routledge & Kegan Paul, p. 82.

Bernstein, B. B. and Young, D. (1967), 'Social Class Differences in Conceptions of the Uses of Toys', *Sociology*, 1, 2.

Blishen, E. (1966), *Roaring Boys*, London, Panther.

Bloom, B. S. *et al.* (1956), *Taxonomy of Educational Objectives: 1. Cognitive Domain*, London, Longmans.

Board of Education (1904), *The Regulations for Secondary Schools*, London, HMSO.

Board of Education (1937), *Handbook of Suggestions*, London, HMSO.

Boden, P. K. (1976), *New Developments in Geography Teaching*, London, Open Books.

Bourdieu, P. (1971), 'Systems of Education and Systems of Thought' in E. Hopper (ed.), *Readings in the Theory of Educational Systems*, London, Hutchinson.

Bourdieu, P. (1973), 'Cultural Reproduction and Social Reproduction' in R. Brown (ed.), *Knowledge, Education and Cultural Change*, London, Tavistock.

Bourdieu, P. (1974), 'The School as a Conservative Force: Scholastic and Cultural Inequalities' in J. Eggleston (ed.), *Contemporary Research in the Sociology of Education*, London, Methuen.

Bourdieu, P. and de Saint-Martin, M. (1974), 'Scholastic Excellence and the Values of the Educational System' in J. Eggleston (ed.), *Contemporary Research in the Sociology of Education*, London, Methuen.

Bourne, D. (1976), 'Education and the Labour Party', unpublished PhD thesis, Keele University.

Bowles, S. and Gintis, H. (1976). *Schooling in Capitalist America*, London, Routledge & Kegan Paul.

Brandis, W. and Henderson, D. (1970), *Social Class, Language and Communication*, London, Routledge & Kegan Paul, pp. 122–3.

Brent, A. (1975), 'The Sociology of Knowledge and Epistemology' in *British Journal of Educational Studies*, 23, 2.

Brock, W. H. (1971), 'Prologue to Heurism', in History of Education Society, *The Changing Curriculum*, London, Methuen.

Bronfenbrenner, U. (1970), *Two Worlds of Childhood: US and USSR*, New York, Russell Sage.

Brown, M. R. (1971), 'Some Strategies used in Primary Schools for Initiating and Implementing Change', Manchester, unpublished M.Ed. thesis.

Bruner, J. S. (1960), *The Process of Instruction*, Cambridge, Massachusetts, Harvard University Press.

Bruner, J. S. (1966), *Towards a Theory of Instruction*, Cambridge, Massachusetts, The Belknap Press.

Calvert, B. (1975), *The Role of the Pupil*, London, Routledge & Kegan Paul.

Campbell, F. (1968), 'Latin and the Elite Tradition in Education', *British Journal of Sociology*, 19, 3, pp. 308−25.

Cantor, L. and Roberts, I. F. (1969), *Further Education in England and Wales*, London, Routledge & Kegan Paul.

Castle, E. B. (1956), *Ancient Education and Today*, Harmondsworth, Penguin.

Cicourel, A. V. and Kitsuse, J. I. (1963), *The Educational Decision Makers*, Indianapolis, Bobbs-Merrill.

Cole, G. D. H. (1935), *A Simple Case for Socialism*, London, Gollancz, p. 252.

Coleman, T. (1968), *The Railway Navvies*, London, Hamish Hamilton.

Cox, C. B. and Dyson, A. (eds) (1971), *The Black Papers on Education 1−3*, London, Davis-Poynter.

Cox, C. B. and Dyson, A. (eds) (1974), *Black Paper No. 4*, London, Dent.

Cox, C. B. and Boyson, R. (eds) (1975), *The Fight for Education*, London, Dent.

Crowther Report (1958), Ministry of Education, *16−18*, London, HMSO.

Cruickshank, M. A. C. (1963), *Church and State in Education*, London, Macmillan.

Cuddihy, R. *et al.* (eds) (1970), *The Red Paper*, Edinburgh, Islander Publications.

Dahrendorf, R. (1960), 'Homo Sociologicus' in *Essays in the Theory of Society*, New York, Wiley, p. 56.

Delamont, S. (1976), *Interaction in the Classroom*, London, Methuen.

Dennis, N., Henriques, F. M. and Slaughter, C. (1957), *Coal Is Our Life*, London, Eyre & Spottiswoode.

Douglas, J. W. B. (1964), *The Home and the School*, London, MacGibbon & Kee.

Dreeben, R. (1967), 'The Contribution of Schooling to the Learning of Norms', *Harvard Educational Review*, 37, 2.

Durkheim, E., trans. Fox, S. D. (1956), *Education and Sociology*, Chicago, Free Press.

Dyson, A. E. (1972), 'The Structures We Need' in R. Boyson (ed.), *Education: Threatened Standards*, Enfield, Churchill, pp. 126−7.

Edmonds, E. L. (1962), *The School Inspector*, London, Routledge & Kegan Paul.

Eggleston, J. (ed.) (1974), *Contemporary Research in the Sociology of Education*, London, Methuen.

Eggleston, J. (1975), 'The Diversification of Post Secondary Education in Europe', *Paedagogica Europaea*, X, 1.

Eggleston, J. (1976a), *Developments in Design Education*, London, Open Books.

Eggleston, J. (1976b), *Adolescence and Identity*, London, Edward Arnold.

Eggleston, J. and Gleeson, D. (1977), 'Curriculum Innovation and the Context of the School', in D. Gleeson (ed.), *Identity and Structure*, Driffield, Nafferton.

Esland, G. M. (1971), 'Teaching and Learning as the Organisation of Knowledge' in M. F. D. Young (ed.), *Knowledge and Control*, London, Collier-Macmillan.

Evetts, J. (1973), *The Sociology of Educational Ideas*, London, Routledge & Kegan Paul.

Freire, P. (1971), *Pedagogy of the Oppressed*, Harmondsworth, Penguin.

Freire, P. (1972), 'Interview with Paullo Freire' in *Times Educational Supplement*, 20 October.

Garfinkel, H. (1967), *Studies in Ethnomethodology*, Englewood Cliffs, New Jersey, Prentice Hall.

Geer, B. (1966), 'Occupational Commitment and the Teaching Profession', *School Review*, 74, 1, pp. 31–47.

Geer, B. (1968), 'Teaching' in *International Encyclopedia of the Social Sciences*, New York, Free Press.

Gleeson, D. (ed.) (1977), *Identity and Structure*, Driffield, Nafferton.

Goffman, E. (1971), *Relations in Public*, Harmondsworth, Penguin.

Goldby, M., Greenwald, J. and West, R. (eds) (1976), *Curriculum Design and Development*, London, Croom Helm.

Gorbutt, D. (1972), 'The New Sociology of Teaching' in *Education for Teaching*, 89.

Halsey, A. H. (1972), *Educational Priority*, London, HMSO.

Hanson, D. (1971), 'The Development of a Professional Association of Art Teachers', *Studies in Design Education*, 3, 2.

Hanson, D. (1973), 'The Royal Wedding Project' in *New Society*, 23 October.

Hargreaves, D. H. (1967), *Social Relations in a Secondary School*, London, Routledge & Kegan Paul.

Hargreaves, D. H. (1972), *Interpersonal Relations and Education*, London, Routledge & Kegan Paul.

Harris, A., Lawn, M. and Prescott, W. (eds) (1976), *Curriculum Innovation*, London, Croom Helm.

Headlam, J. W. (1902), *General Reports on Higher Education: The Teaching of Literary Subjects in some Secondary Schools*, London, Board of Education.

Henry, J. (1960), 'A Cross Cultural Outline of Education', *Current Anthropology*, 1, 4.

Hirst, P. H. (1965), 'Morals, Religion and the Maintained School', *British Journal of Educational Studies*, XIV, 1.

Hirst, P. H. (1975), *Knowledge and the Curriculum*, London, Routledge & Kegan Paul.

Hobsbawm, E. J. (1956), *The Labour Aristocracy*, London, Lawrence & Wishart.

Hoggart, R. (1960), *The Uses of Literacy*, Harmondsworth, Penguin.

Holly, D. (1973), *Beyond Curriculum*, London, Hart-Davis MacGibbon.

Holt, J. (1964), *Why Children Fail*, London, Pitman.

Hoyle, E. (1969a), 'How Does the Curriculum Change? 1. A Proposal for Enquiries', *Journal of Curriculum Studies*, 1, 2.

Hoyle, E. (1969b), 'How Does the Curriculum Change? 2. Systems and Strategies', *Journal of Curriculum Studies*, 1, 3.

Hoyle, E. (1971), *Personal Relationships and the Management of Schools*, unpublished paper presented to National Association of Schoolmasters Annual Conference.

Hoyle, E. (1972), *Creativity in the School*, Paris, OECD mimeo.

Hurd, G. E. and Johnson, T. F. (1967), 'Education and Development', *Sociological Review*, 15, 1.

Hurt, J. S. (1970), *Education in Evolution*, London, Hart-Davis.

Illich, I. (1971), *Deschooling Society*, London, Calder & Boyars.

Incorporated Association of Assistant Masters (1900), *Circular to Members*.

Jackson, P. W. (1968), *Life in Classrooms*, New York, Holt, Rinehart & Winston.

Jencks, C. (1972), *Inequality; A Reassessment of the Effect of Family and Schooling in America*, London, Allen Lane.

Jenkins, D. and Shipman, M. D. (1976), *Curriculum: An Interaction*, London, Open Books.

Keddie, N. (1971), 'Classroom Knowledge' in M. F. D. Young (ed.), *Knowledge and Control*, London, Collier-Macmillan, pp. 139–40, 155.

Keddie, N. (ed.) (1973), *Tinker, Tailor. . . . The Myth of Cultural Deprivation*, Harmondsworth, Penguin.

Kerr, J. F. (1967), *The Problem of Curriculum Reform*, Leicester, University Press.

Kuhn, T. S. (1970), *The Structure of Scientific Revolutions*, University of Chicago Press.

Labov, W. (1969), 'The Logic of Non-Standard English' in J. Alatis (ed.), *School of Languages and Linguistics Monograph*, Series No. 22, Georgetown University Press.

Lacey, C. (1970), *Hightown Grammar: The School as a Social System*, Manchester University Press.

Lawton, D. (1975), *Class, Culture and the Curriculum*, London, Routledge & Kegan Paul.

Lee, D. J. (1968), 'Class Differentials in Educational Opportunity and Promotions from the Ranks', *Sociology*, 2, 3.

Little, A. and Westergaard, J. (1964), 'The Trend of Class Differentials in Educational Opportunity in England and Wales', *British Journal of Sociology*, 15, 4.

Livingstone, R. W. (1916), *A Defence of Classical Education*, London, Macmillan.

Lowndes, G. A. N. (1969), *The Silent Social Revolution* (2nd edn), Oxford University Press.

Macdonald, B. (1973), 'Innovation and Incompetence' in D. Hamingson (ed.), *Towards Judgement: the Publications of the Evaluation Unit of the Humanities Curriculum Project 1970–1972*, Norwich, Centre for Applied Research in Education.

McGregor, L. (1976), *New Developments in Drama Teaching*, London, Open Books.

Mackenzie, G. N. (1964), 'Curricular Change' in M. B. Miles (ed.), *Innovation in Education*, New York, Teachers College, Columbia.

McTavish, J. (1916), *What Labour Wants from Education*, London, WEA, p. 5.

Mannheim, K. (1936), *Ideology and Utopia: An Introduction to the Sociology of Knowledge*, London, Routledge & Kegan Paul.

Manzer, R. A. (1970), *Teachers and Politics*, Manchester University Press.

Marshall, S. (1968), *Adventures in Creative Education*, Oxford, Pergamon.

Marx, K. and Engels, F. (1964), *The German Ideology*, London, Lawrence & Wishart.

Mead, M. (1951), *The School in American Culture*, Cambridge, Mass., Harvard University Press.

Merton, R. K. (1968), *Social Theory and Social Structure*, New York, Free Press.

Ministry of Education (1947a), *Handbook of Suggestions for Teachers*, London, HMSO.

Ministry of Education (1947b), *The New Secondary Education* (Pamphlet No. 9), London, HMSO.

Ministry of Education (1959), *Primary Education*, London, HMSO.

Mothersole, P. (1975), 'Publishing and the Schools Council' in *The Schools Council: A Second Look*, London, Ward Lock.

Musgrave, P. W. (1967), *Technical Change, the Labour Force and Education*, Oxford, Pergamon.

Musgrave, P. W. (1971), 'Towards a Sociology of the Curriculum', *Paedagogica Europaea*, VI.

Musgrave, P. W. (1972), 'Social Factors affecting the Curriculum', in P. W. Hughes (ed.), *The Teacher's Role in Curriculum Design*, London, Angus & Richardson.

Musgrave, P. W. (1973), *Knowledge, Curriculum and Change*, London, Angus & Robertson.

Musgrove, F. (1964), *Youth and the Social Order*, London, Routledge & Kegan Paul.

Musgrove, F. (1968), 'The Contribution of Sociology to the Study of the Curriculum' in J. F. Kerr (ed.), *Changing the Curriculum*, London, University of London Press.

Musgrove, F. and Taylor, P. H. (1969), *Society and the Teacher's Role*, London, Routledge & Kegan Paul.

Nash, R. (1974), 'Camouflage in the Classroom', in J. Eggleston (ed.), *Contemporary Research in the Sociology of Education*, London, Methuen.

National Association for the Teaching of English (1964), *The Organisation and Atmosphere of School*, p. 11.

Neave, G. (1975), *How They Fared*, London, Routledge & Kegan Paul.

Newsom Report (1963), Ministry of Education, *All Our Future*, London, HMSO.

Observer (1968), 15 September, quoted by J. S. Hurt (1971), *Education in Evolution*, London, Hart-Davis, p. 13.

Open University (1972), *The Curriculum: Context Design and Development E283 Units 1–12*, Milton Keynes, Open University Press.

Owen, J. G. (1973), *The Management of Curriculum Development*, Cambridge University Press.

Parlett, M. and Hamilton, D. (1972), *Evaluation as Illumination: A new approach to the study of innovating programmes*, Edinburgh, Centre for Research in the Educational Sciences, mimeo.

Parsons, T. (1961), 'The School Class as a Social System' in A. H. Halsey, J. Floud and C. A. Anderson (eds), *Education Economy and Society*, New York, Free Press, pp. 434–55.

Peters, R. S. (ed.) (1973), 'The Justification of Education' in *Oxford Readings in Philosophy: Philosophy of Education*, Oxford University Press.

Phenix, P. H. (1962), 'The Disciplines as Curriculum Content' in A. H. Passow (ed.), *Curriculum Crossroads*, New York, Teachers' College Press.

Phenix, P. H. (1964a), 'The Architectonics of Knowledge' in S. Elam (ed.), *Education and the Structure of Knowledge*, Chicago, Rand McNally.

Phenix, P. H. (1964b), *Realms of Meaning*, New York, McGraw-Hill.

Phillips, D. Z. (1970), 'Philosophy and Religious Education', *British Journal of Educational Studies*, XVIII, 1.

Piaget, J. (1958), *The Development of Logical Thinking from Childhood to Adolescence*, London, Routledge & Kegan Paul.

Postman, N. and Weingartner, C. (1971), *Teaching as a Subversive Activity*, Harmondsworth, Penguin.

Reimer, E. (1971), *School Is Dead*, Harmondsworth, Penguin.

Richardson, E. (1973), *The Teacher, the School and the Task of Management*, London, Heinemann.

Rist, R. (1970), 'Student Social Class and Teacher Expectation', *Harvard Educational Review*, 40, 30, pp. 411, 451.

Robinson, P. E. D. R. (1974), 'An Ethnography of Classrooms' in J. Eggleston (ed.), *Contemporary Research in the Sociology of Education*, London, Methuen.

Rosenthal, R. and Jacobson, L. (1968), *Pygmalion in the Classroom*, New York, Holt, Rinehart & Winston.

Rubinstein, D. and Stoneman, C. (eds) (1970), *Education for Democracy*, Harmondsworth, Penguin.

Sand, O. (1968), reported in J. S. McClure (ed.), *Curriculum Innovation in Practice*, London, HMSO, p. 30.

Schools Council Art Committee (1975), Evidence to working party on 16 Whole Curriculum. Mimeo, unpublished. The evidence is used in Schools Council (1975).

Schools Council (1968), *Society and the Young School Leaver*, London, HMSO.

Schools Council (1969), *Young School Leavers*, London, HMSO.

Schools Council (1973), 'Submission of Art Committee to Working Party on the Whole Curriculum', unpublished mimeo.

Schools Council (1974), *Social Education: An Experiment in Four Secondary Schools*, Working Paper 51, London, Evans/Methuen Educational.

Schools Council (1975), *The Whole Curriculum 13–16*, Working Paper No. 53, London, Evans/Methuen Educational.

Schutz, A. (1967), *Collected Papers*, Vol. 1, The Hague, Martinus Nijhoff.

Sharp, R. and Green, A. G. (1975), *Education and Social Control*, London, Routledge & Kegan Paul.

Shipman, M. D. (1971), *Education and Modernisation*, London, Faber.

Shipman, M. D. (1974), 'The Impact of a Curriculum Project' in J. Eggleston (ed.), *Contemporary Research in the Sociology of Education*, London, Methuen.

Shipman, M. D., Bolam, D. and Jenkins, D. (1974), *Inside a Curriculum Project*, London, Methuen.

Silver, H. (1973), *Equal Opportunity in Education*, London, Methuen.

Smith, D. (1971), 'Selection and Knowledge Management in Educational Systems' in E. Hopper (ed.), *Readings in the Theory of Educational Systems*, London, Hutchinson.

Smith, D. (1976), 'Codes, Paradigms and Folk Norms', *Sociology*, 10, 1.

Stenhouse, L. (1975), *An Introduction to Curriculum Research and Development*, London, Heinemann.

Stevens, F. (1960), *The Living Tradition*, London, Hutchinson.

Stewart, W. A. C. (1972), *Progressives and Radicals in English Education 1750–1970*, London, Macmillan.

Stubbs, M. (1976), *Language, Schools and Classrooms*, London, Methuen.

Swift, D. F. (1964), 'Who Passes the Eleven Plus', *New Society*, 5 March.

Tawney, R. H. (1922), *Secondary Education for All*, London, Allen & Unwin.

Taylor, P. H., Reid, W. A., Holley, B. J. and Exon, G. (1974), *Purpose, Power and Constraint in the Primary School Curriculum*, London, Macmillan.

Taylor, P. H., Reid, W. A. and Holley, B. J. (1974), *The English Sixth Form: A Case Study in Curriculum Research*, London, Routledge & Kegan Paul.

Taylor, R. W. (1949), *Basic Principles of Curriculum and Instruction*, University of Chicago Press.

Taylor, W. (1963), *The Secondary Modern School*, London, Faber.

Taylor, W. (1969), *Society and the Education of Teachers*, London, Faber.

The Teacher (1964), 'Schools Council: why there are reservations', editorial comment, 20 March, p. 22.

The Teacher (1975), 'Teacher Critic Suspended', 12 September, p. 1.

Thompson, E. P. (1968), *The Making of the English Working Class*, Harmondsworth, Penguin.

Thring, E. (1867), *Education and the School*, London, Macmillan, p. 39.

Tyler, W. (1977), *Language, Schools and Classrooms*, London, Methuen.

Vallance, E. (1973), 'Hiding the Hidden Curriculum', *Curriculum Theory Network*, 4, 1.

Vaughan, M. and Archer, M. S. (1971), *Social Conflict and Educational Change in England and France 1789–1848*, Cambridge University Press.

Vulliamy, G. (1976), 'What Counts as School Music' in G. Whitty and M. F. D. Young (eds), *Explorations in the Sociology and Politics of School Knowledge*, Driffield, Nafferton.

Waller, W. (1932), *The Sociology of Teaching*, New York, Wiley.

Warner, W. L., Havighurst, R. J. and Loeb, M. B. (1946), *Who Shall Be Educated?*, London, Kegan Paul.

Watson, F. R. (1976), *New Developments in Mathematics Teaching*, London, Open Books.

Wax, M. L. and Wax, R. H. (1964), 'Formal Education in an American Indian Community', *Social Problems Monographs*, No. 2.

Wax, M. L. and Wax, R. H. (1973) in N. Keddie (ed.), *Tinker, Tailor . . . The Myth of Cultural Deprivation*, Harmondsworth, Penguin.

Webb, J. (1962), 'The Sociology of a School', *British Journal of Sociology*, 13, 2.

Webster, C. (1971), 'The Scholastic Curriculum from 1640–1660' in History of Education Society, *The Changing Curriculum*, London, Methuen.

Webster, C. (1975), 'The Curriculum of the Grammar Schools and Universities 1500–1600: A critical review of the literature', *History of Education*, 4, 1.

Wells, H. G. (1917), 'The Case Against Classical Languages', *Fortnightly Review*, April.

White, J. P. (1968), 'Instruction in Obedience', *New Society*, 2 May.

White, J. P. (1973), *Towards a Compulsory Curriculum*, London, Routledge & Kegan Paul.

Whitfield, R. C. (ed.) (1971), *Disciplines of the Curriculum*, New York, McGraw-Hill.

Whitty, G. and Young, M. (1976), *Exploration in the Politics of School Knowledge*, Driffield, Nafferton.

Wilkinson, R. H. (1964), *The Prefects: British Leadership and the Public School Tradition. A Comparative Study in the Making of Rulers*, Oxford University Press.

Williams, R. (1961), *The Long Revolution*, London, Chatto & Windus.

Williams, W. and Rennie, J. (1972), 'Social Education' in D. Rubinstein and C. Stoneman (eds), *Education for Democracy*, 2nd edn, Harmondsworth, Penguin.

Young, M. F. D. (ed.) (1971), *Knowledge and Control*, London, Collier-Macmillan.

Young, M. F. D. (1972), 'On the Politics of Educational Knowledge', *Economy and Society*, 11, 2.

Index

For full bibliographical details of works referred to in the index by author and date, see the bibliography.

Figures in **bold type** indicate more important references.